estherpress

Books for Courageous Women

ESTHER PRESS VISION

Publishing diverse voices that encourage and equip women to walk courageously in the light of God's truth for such a time as this.

BIBLICAL STATEMENT OF PURPOSE

"For if you remain silent at this time, relief and deliverance for the Jews will arise from another place, but you and your father's family will perish. And who knows but that you have come to your royal position for such a time as this?"

– Esther 4:14

What people are saying about …

STAND IN CONFIDENCE

"The truth is, we have cultivated a generation of insecure Christians who are clamoring for influence and accolades instead of completely surrendering to a God who not only supplies all our needs but also gives us the confidence to experience secure joy in our walks with Him and in our callings from Him. In *Stand in Confidence*, Amanda takes on the hard but holy work of teaching a transformational framework that reshapes our identities and then vulnerably shows us how to do it well."

Toni J. Collier, founder of Broken Crayons,
author of *Brave Enough to Be Broken*

"Amanda reminds us that false beliefs about ourselves create a future beneath ourselves. *Stand in Confidence* shows us that in order to shift into God's bigger plan and purpose, we must dare to create a new inner narrative to enter an anointed, next-level future. A bold, vulnerable, and necessary read."

Marshawn Evans Daniels, TV
personality, reinvention strategist for
women, founder of SheProfits.com

"Amanda does a beautiful job of marrying our need for security and confidence with the beauty of the gospel and full reliance on Jesus. It's one thing to say your confidence comes from Christ but another to show someone how. This is exactly what this book does, and I'm thankful so many will be able to read it!"

Chelsea Hurst, author of *Your Own Beautiful* and *Above All Else*

"Amanda Pittman gives us powerful strategies to defeat lies, change our thinking, and stand in confidence with God's truth."

Ashley "Empowers" Brown, CEO and founder of The High Earning Housewife

"Amanda constantly and consistently shares the power and promises of Jesus. She is a truth teller who is always pointing back to the ultimate Power Source. If you're looking for a manual for uncovering your God-given identity and connecting with Him on a deeper level, this is it. Amanda writes from hard-earned experience and shares practical wisdom to help you not only be inspired but EQUIPPED to walk your own path toward bold confidence in all that you do."

Hannah Brencher, author of *Fighting Forward* and *Come Matter Here*

"In *Stand in Confidence*, Amanda offers an honest voice on the journey to living an empowered life, rooted in faith and bringing clarity and practical guidance on how to get there. Readers are invited to ground themselves in an internal security in an ever-changing world, particularly in an age of social media comparison, where many have felt too paralyzed by doubt to show up for the calling on their lives. I can't think of a better time for our generation to embrace this message. It's vulnerable, it's real, and it challenges us in all the right places."

Brittney Moses, author of *Worthy: 50 Mindful Moments to Bring Clarity and Peace to Your Day*

STAND IN

CONFIDENCE

Amanda Pittman

STAND IN

CONFIDENCE

From Sinking in Insecurity
to Rising in Your
God-Given Identity

estherpress

Books for Courageous Women
from David C Cook

STAND IN CONFIDENCE
Published by David C Cook
4050 Lee Vance Drive
Colorado Springs, CO 80918 U.S.A.

Integrity Music Limited, a Division of David C Cook
Brighton, East Sussex BN1 2RE, England

The graphic circle C logo is a registered trademark of David C Cook.

The website addresses recommended throughout this book are offered as a
resource to you. These websites are not intended in any way to be or imply an
endorsement on the part of David C Cook, nor do we vouch for their content.

Details in some stories have been changed to protect the identities of the persons involved.

Library of Congress Control Number 2022933401
ISBN 978-0-8307-8441-7
eISBN 978-0-8307-8442-4

The Team: Susan McPherson, Stephanie Bennett, Julie Cantrell,
Judy Gillispie, James Hershberger, Susan Murdock
Cover Design: James Hershberger

Printed in the United States of America
First Edition 2022

1 2 3 4 5 6 7 8 9 10

060122

CONTENTS

FOREWORD

"You have thunder thighs," I heard as her words reverberated through my teenage brain, making their way from my ears straight to my heart. My athletic legs had been an insecurity of mine from the time I was a little girl and first became aware of my body compared to other girls' bodies.

I dreaded dressing rooms. When Mom would take us on our annual back-to-school shopping trip to try on new pants, the mirrors in those tiny little rooms always seemed to be a reminder that my legs were "bigger" than the other girls'.

So when the mean girl put words to my biggest insecurity at the time, I wholeheartedly believed it. It didn't matter that she had a reputation for putting others down or that my legs were actually totally fine. I couldn't see that then. And her flippant insult felt like confirmation of everything I didn't like about my body and of what I worried others were secretly thinking when they looked at me. Confidence status: crushed.

If only I could have gone back and whispered to my younger self, "That's a lie from the pit of hell," perhaps I could have saved myself years of trying to compensate for confidence, which led to all sorts of brokenness, from disordered eating to seeking the attention of boys to burning myself out as I hustled after accolades and approval.

Though I'm not sure I would have believed my older, wiser self anyway. Back then, my confidence didn't rest in the finished work of Christ. It rested in myself. I mean, I knew about God. I went to church. But I didn't know my identity. So when anything or anyone seemed to point out my insecurities, I'd crumble and try to compensate. Why? Because identity—a secure identity in Christ—is the remedy to insecurity. Without it, we seek stability and security in literally everything we think will help but that ultimately cannot deliver: relationships, approval, status, appearance, money, achievement, and more.

Each of these things seems to promise confidence only to almost always leave us more insecure than before. These things are fleeting. Praise God there is something more lasting, true, and eternally reliable to place our confidence in: the finished work of Christ.

That sounds super Christiany, and I know in saying it, I sound a little like the cheesy counselor from summer church camp. Because while we may know in our heads it's true, the question that naturally comes next is, "How? How do I actually do that?"

How do we not just hear and know it in our heads but also know it in our hearts? Allow it to seep into every cell of our being and change literally everything, as we've so often been told it has the power to do?

It's an honest question. One I've asked before. And I'm sure one you've wondered as well. Aside from being a cliché Christian saying, what can embracing our true identity and finding confidence in Christ actually look like? In practice. In the real moments of life. When someone insults us. When we don't like how the image in the mirror appears. When we fall short of our goals.

That's what Amanda shows us how to do in these pages. Instead of just telling you what you may have heard a million times, she's written a road map with practical application so that you don't only hear *what* you need to know but also actually know *how* to live like it's true.

It's time for us as women in the modern world to quit relying on cliché Instagram graphics to get our confidence fix. It's time to stop saying or reposting things we don't even know how to live or if we believe. It's time for us to rise up and truly learn how to find confidence in Christ and live like we mean what we say we believe.

And this book? These pages? This is where we start.

Jordan Lee Dooley
bestselling author, podcaster,
founder of Own It Academy and SoulScripts

TAKE A STAND

On a recent trip down memory lane, I was scrolling my Facebook timeline. I made it all the way back in the archives to my high school posts.

So. Much. Cringe.

The old statuses showed a diverse portfolio of indie song lyrics, poetic quotes (to make me sound deep), and lots of teenage angst with pinches of rage and cussing sprinkled throughout. As I was scrolling, one post stopped me dead in my tracks.

It read, "I feel like my insecurities get in the way of everything in my life."

My jaw dropped.

I could still remember how that insecurity felt. I remembered the crippling shame. Never feeling good enough. Feeling as if there were holes in the bucket of my soul. No matter how much love or affirmation poured in, it would inevitably drip out and leave me hungry for more.

This insecurity kept me in relationships that I never should have entertained and kept me away from opportunities that I should have explored.

Yet there I was, more than a decade later, leading a ministry called Confident Woman Co. and equipping other women to stand confidently upon the finished work of Jesus. And there I was—a confident woman—after many painful years of sinking in insecurity.

That's why this book exists.

From my years leading and mentoring Christian women, I've seen far too many downgrade their identity and dismiss their authority because of sinking insecurity.

Society has conditioned many of us to believe false narratives about who we're supposed to be. In time, we can begin to think that if we play the part well enough, *then* we'll gain love, acceptance, validation, and significance. But the rules are always changing, so we don't know who to be or what to do from one day to the next. As a result, the insecurity drives us to people-please, downplay, settle, and perform.

This can even be the fruit of what we learn in church. Many churches beat the dead horse about how lost, depraved, and powerless we are without Christ while failing to be just as loud about how righteous, sanctified, and empowered we are through Him.

I mean, isn't *that* the good news we should be talking about?

The inevitable result of society's disqualifying beliefs is defeated behavior. How sad!

Rather than standing confidently in our identity as daughters of God and co-heirs with Christ, we sink in insecurity.

It's more than a shame. It's a tragedy.

In this book we will challenge the false narratives and explore the tools you need to write a new story. A true story.

Why? Because that's what God wants for you. He even tells us in the Scriptures. Romans 5:2 says, "Because of our faith, Christ has brought us into this place of undeserved privilege where we now stand, and we **confidently** and joyfully look forward to sharing God's glory."

See? Faith in Christ brings us into a place of privilege. **Confidence.** And joy! I've found that spiritual confidence, and now it's time for YOU to access everything that Jesus came to give you. Once you start standing confidently in *your* God-given identity, there'll be no limit to what you can do with your life.

FAITH IN CHRIST BRINGS US INTO A PLACE OF PRIVILEGE. *CONFIDENCE.* AND JOY!

With a firm foundation underfoot, you'll no longer sabotage the abundant life God has planned for you. God will bring overflow to your life ... more than enough to share with others. And as those blessings are given to you, you'll confidently receive and multiply the good for God's glory.

Are you wondering how to make all this happen?

In *Stand in Confidence*, I'll walk you through the **Four Components of Confidence** so that you can become the spiritually confident woman God intended you to be.

Four Components of Confidence

CLARITY   CONNECTION   COMPETENCY   CONVICTION

1. **Clarity**—Embrace your identity and define your design.
2. **Connection**—Connect with God and connect with others.
3. **Competency**—Expand your capacity and sharpen your ability.
4. **Conviction**—Know your responsibility and use your authority.

These four pillars, when working together, will create a framework for rock-solid confidence.

You have work to do, and some of it won't come easily. But the good news is you're not alone in this spiritual journey. I'm giving you the blueprint that led me to Christ-centered confidence, and more importantly, God is guiding you every step of the way.

Are you ready to stop sinking in the sands of insecurity so you can stand on the rocks of spiritual confidence?

Let's dig in.

Clarity

COMPONENT OF CONFIDENCE #1

Searching for Answers

As the chill of the October breeze grazed my face, I sat on the patio weeping. Wiping my cheeks with the sleeve of my neon-green sweater, the tears fell faster than I was able to catch them.

Through the computer screen, my therapist looked at me with compassion in her eyes. She wanted to know what had triggered such an emotional overspill.

I struggled to gather my swirling thoughts. Since starting counseling with Mrs. Jay, I'd been yearning for something I couldn't quite name. I hadn't realized it until this exact moment, but I had been searching for one piece of clarity.

My hope had been set on her unearthing lost memories out of the crevices of my soul, piecing them together into a sequential life-masterpiece, and delivering a transformational "aha!" moment in which I could clearly say, "Yes! There it is!"

There's the thing.

There's the reason.

There's the moment.

There's *The Answer.*

I was sobbing on the porch that day because I'd finally realized that I already had The Answer. After all, The Answer was the very belief I'd professed to live by as a "mature" Christian. Even more, it's what I had long been preaching about in my ministry.

All that time I had known The Answer, but now it seemed clear that I had never fully *believed* it. Otherwise, I wouldn't have been looking in all directions for a truth I'd already found. While Mrs. Jay had been helpful and insightful, I realized that I had been rummaging through the wisdom of another human being to discover that, despite Mrs. Jay's training and credentials and experience, she had nothing more than Christ to offer me.

But she did help me understand that I already knew The Answer: Jesus.

The Answer was Jesus.

It always had been and forever will be Jesus.

At first, I wanted to find some practical, psychological, or emotional counterpart to support The Answer. But rather than mining the answers from within myself, as if I were some omniscient source of meaning and reason, I learned, with Mrs. Jay's help, to weigh my experiences by Scripture.

As I came to the end of myself time and time again, whether on my own or with Mrs. Jay's guidance, I always found Him. Only Him.

That day she helped me see that:

I suffer because Jesus suffered.

I get rejected because Jesus was rejected.

I am tested because Jesus was tested.

I will be betrayed because Jesus was betrayed.

And if these things are true, then others must be true too:

If I'm rejected like Him, then I'll also be accepted by the Father like Him.

If I'm betrayed like Him, then I'll also be elevated like Him.

If I'm tested like Him, then I'll also be proven like Him.

If I suffer like Him, then I will also be glorified like Him.

What I gained that day in therapy with Mrs. Jay was *certainty*—certainty that Jesus is The Answer and that His unshakable foundation of truth is strong enough to support me. This newfound clarity was my first step in learning to stand in confidence, and it became the footing upon which all the other layers were built.

Clarify Who You Are in Christ

Clarity is the first component of confidence. The more clarity you have about who you are, why you're here, and what you're designed to do, the more confident you'll be. Plus, when you know who you are, you'll know what to do—because out of who you are flows what you do.

Therefore, this section of the book will be broken into two chapters:

> ▸ **Embrace Your Identity** | Know Who You Are
> ▸ **Define Your Design** | Know What to Do

As you embrace your identity in Christ and define your God-given design, you'll develop the clarity to move forward in confidence.

Chapter 1

EMBRACE YOUR IDENTITY

Lay a Foundation of Love

When constructing a house, the foundation is the most expensive part of the process. If the foundation is off, the entire structure is off. A beautiful house can have custom cabinets, sparkling floors, and expensive decor, but if the foundation is faulty …

Walls will crack.

Floors will sag.

Rooms will shift.

Doors won't shut.

Scale matters too. Laying the foundation of a house may take three weeks to complete, but laying the foundation of a skyscraper can take more than three months.

The taller you want to build, the deeper you need to dig.

At some point in life, we may begin to think we're too far along in our faith journey to focus on our spiritual foundation. We think we've learned all there is to know about God, and we take the love of Christ for granted, forgetting it is the vital rock upon which we stand.

THE TALLER YOU WANT TO BUILD, THE DEEPER YOU NEED TO DIG.

"Jesus loves you" becomes a sweet saying we teach our children in Sunday school, but we forget to share the same message with grown-ups on Sunday mornings, launching into dramatic stories of the four horsemen or doomsday prophecies instead. If we aren't careful, we can even begin to trust in some minister's spectacle of deliverance, attaching our faith to the weekly rituals and forgetting that Christ's love is most important.

Don't get me wrong, it's essential to be biblically literate. And, of course, there's a time and a place for deliverance. But the moment that pride puffs up in our hearts and we say, "Oh, I've made it! I'm a mature Christian. I already know the gospel. I don't need to read that anymore!"—that's when we're most susceptible to fall.

Hear this: God has a great plan for your life. But remember, the higher you're going to build, the deeper you need to go.

In other words, if you have a huge call on your life, then your foundation needs to become MORE secure, not less. Think of love—God's love—as the steady concrete base that supports your confidence. We need to pay close attention to building and maintaining that foundation so we can grow to reach our greatest potential in life.

REFLECT + PRAY

Reflect

- In what areas of your life do you find it most challenging to trust that God's love can support you?
- In what areas have you searched for confidence apart from Jesus?

Pray

- Pray for a deeper revelation of the certainty, reliability, and power of Jesus.
- Ask Him to meet you with truth, wisdom, and understanding in the areas where you've searched for confidence apart from Him.
- Write down anything He calls to your attention.

Faulty Love

In my younger years, a faulty foundation of love led to my own collapse. You see, I had a boyfriend in high school who was a destiny destroyer. By offering me attention and affirmation, he rewarded me with what I lacked and wanted most in my life. And because I had little self-worth at that time, I became hooked on him like a drug.

Once I took the bait, he moved quickly.

Only weeks into the relationship, he shifted from the love-bombing phase and began requesting withdrawals from the love bank. He would constantly ask for sexual favors, emotionally coercing me into action by suggesting that if I refused his requests, then I must not truly love him. Time after time, he would compliment my appearance, my curves, my sex appeal. If I gave him what he wanted, he made me feel desired, pursued, and worthy.

I was young, naive, and desperate for approval. So I compromised my beliefs and values to gain his affirmation. Needless to say, he broke every boundary I set, yet my need for his "love" kept me chained. I was objectified for my features and pressured to send seductive pictures. He rewarded me with praise when I complied. If I said no, he withdrew his affection and attention to punish me, leaving me feeling unwanted and unworthy.

This toxic cycle was the open door that Satan used to distort my view of love. I began to intertwine value, worthiness, and love with sex, appearance, and performance.

This sent one strong message: love is transactional.

Transactional Love

"I would never stay in a relationship if a guy was unfaithful," I'd always vowed. But in time, the trauma bonds that developed within this unhealthy relationship had led me to become a person I swore I'd never be. I'd built my life upon the unstable foundation of transactional love, and those shifting sands kept me jumping through harder and harder hoops, trying again and again to earn my boyfriend's love.

When the news of his cheating came out, the other girl called me and told me everything. The evidence against him was staggering.

But even though I'd promised myself I would never tolerate such a twisted, sick love story, I still hung on. I was so insecure and broken by that time that I thought settling for scraps was all I was worth. Sadly, revenge became my goal. I wanted to do to him what he had done to me—make him earn my acceptance, approval, and love.

I was no longer the one being hurt. I became the one causing the hurt. I had sunk to my lowest level, all because my shifting foundation of lies could not support me.

The rest of the toxic relationship was spent with him begging for my mercy and me emotionally torturing him for the pain he'd caused me. I even cheated on him for revenge. The transaction progressed to my boyfriend getting his sexual fixes and me getting my emotional vengeance. But, as you might imagine, this pursuit of revenge only pierced an even deeper wound in my soul.

By the time we finally ended our dysfunctional relationship, I was shattered and insecure. The unhealthy experience had skewed my view of everyone—men, who were untrustworthy sexual dogs; women, who were untrustworthy sexual objects; and God, who was an untrustworthy, absent father.

Even worse, the lens through which I viewed the world had become very dark. Blinded by bitterness, I saw the worst in everything and everyone. Tainted by trauma, I abandoned all hope in genuine love. I'd learned the hard way that love was traumatic. Abusive. Manipulative. Compromising. Painful. Demanding. Selfish. Temporary.

And yet, even though I held these new negative beliefs about love, love was still what I craved most.

Mistakenly, I transferred my ex-boyfriend's sin onto God. I charged a holy, blameless God for all the trauma that an immature human had caused me.

How dare God allow me to experience so much pain? I thought to myself, neglecting the protective warnings He had given me throughout the Bible.

I assumed that God couldn't have been "good" if He'd put me through so much heartache. Failing to take responsibility for my own actions, my view of God became skewed—not because of what God had done to me, but because of what a teenage boy had done to me.

Relearning True Love

Not only did this failed romance distort my view of God, but it also distorted my view of marriage.

Fast-forward to my sophomore year of college. The closer God drew me to Him, the more highly I viewed myself and the more accurately I assessed my relationships. This helped me gain the courage to end the relationship with the guy who had bulldozed my self-esteem for years. This breakup was long overdue.

Soon after, a handsome engineering major named Michael scooped up my phone number and started pursuing me. We spent the following winter break on a texting spree, professed our feelings for one another, and became *Facebook official* at the top of spring semester. There was about a month-and-a-half turnaround from the end of my last relationship to the start of my new one.

Let it be known that I don't share this story *proudly*. Entertaining a new prospect immediately after a failed relationship isn't exactly good advice. I tell everyone that God worked it out for me *despite* my choices, not *because* of them. Descriptive, not prescriptive.

That being said, Michael is the single individual who changed me forever. His presence in my life set a new standard for love.

For once in my life, I had firsthand experience with someone who did relationships the right way. And not just our relationship … **every** relationship. Most of all, he treated me with the utmost dignity and respect.

While I had been well versed in the "highly effective" conflict resolution skills of the silent treatment, raising my voice, overreacting, and playing the "guess my feelings" game … he wouldn't even hold a conversation with me unless we both maintained a controlled pace, an indoor voice, and respectful exchanges. He taught me to "use my words" instead of reacting in anger.

Who knew there could be another way? A *better* way?

The most powerful thing this relationship accomplished was expanding my belief of what love could be. Michael broke all the rules I had been taught. He showed me that relationships didn't have to be an emotional roller coaster. They could be a cruise. Hard times didn't have to ruin us. They could actually sharpen us. He wasn't perfect, nor was I. But we *loved* each other well.

Marrying Michael ten months later, when he was twenty-one and I was twenty, was a no-brainer, but the process of restoring my view of myself, reconstructing my view of God, and renewing my view of love would take some time.

When Michael and I first started dating each other, I still had some baggage from that previous relationship. Because of the years of indoctrination, I was convinced that love was dependent on how I performed or looked. I thought I only deserved love if I was beautiful enough, intriguing enough, and accommodating enough to earn it.

Sometimes I would even ask Michael, "Why do you love me?"

Shamelessly fishing for a compliment, I'd expect him to say, "I love you because you're so different from all those other girls. There's nobody like you. Nobody has your smile. You're the only one who gets me. You're my soul mate."

But is that what he said?

Nope.

In fact, when we were engaged, Michael wrote a whole blog about this. And do you know what the title was? "Why I Don't Love My Fiance."[1]

Shocking, right?

Here's a snippet of what he posted:

I don't love Amanda for what's on the outside. *I know. It sounds cheesy, it sounds sappy. This perspective is not a novel idea by any means. How many times have you heard someone say, "I don't love you for what's on the outside. I love you for what's on the inside." But that brings me to my second conclusion.*

I don't love Amanda for what's on the inside *either.*

*   …*

I love her because I choose to.

Loved Despite Yourself

I'll be honest. I didn't like Michael's post.

"What do you mean you choose to love me?" I complained to myself. "Am I so hard to love that you have to have this conversation with yourself, like 'All right, Michael. She's a little crazy and her hiccups sound like a dying cat, but we'll tough it out. Let's just CHOOSE to love Amanda.'"

I was missing the entire point.

First John 4:10 reads, "This is real love—not that we loved God, but that he loved us and sent his Son as a sacrifice to take away our sins."

Likewise, in John 15:16, Jesus says, "You did not choose me, but I chose you" (NIV).

The Bible brings this point home time and time again:

We are only able to love God because He first loved us.

We are only able to choose God because He first chose us.

We're made worthy because the Worthy One first pursued us.

We're made lovable because the Loving One first loved us.

Being married to Michael was but a microcosm of how deep the love of God truly is. It foreshadowed how I would one day fully embrace and accept being loved despite myself, not because of myself.

While I was dating and engaged, I didn't particularly like Michael saying, "I love you because I choose to," but I really liked it once we got married. I liked knowing he chose me, time and again, not only during the good times but also:

> When we got into tough disagreements.
> When I gained weight with my pregnancies.
> When I chopped off my hair and went through the awkward phase.
> When raising kids became extremely challenging.
> When we went through seasons of financial hardship.

As a result of Michael's unconditional and steady love for me, I learned something. God's love—agape love—isn't based on how great we are. It's based on how great GOD is. When I finally understood, accepted, and embraced this truth, my confidence changed, not only in my relationship with God but also in my relationship with Michael.

Identified by Love

Romans 5:8 says,

> God demonstrates his own love for us in this: While we were still sinners, Christ died for us. (NIV)

Read that again.

Let it sink in.

Jesus died for us BEFORE we loved Him, BEFORE we devoted our lives to Him, BEFORE we did anything to earn His love. His love for us always has been and always will be unconditional.

Here's what you need to hold on to: We're not chosen because of what we have done. We're chosen because of what *Christ* has done.

First John 4:9 says, "This is how God showed his love among us: He sent his one and only Son into the world that we might live through him" (NIV).

This. Is. Love! Not that we loved God, but that He loved us and sent His Son as an atoning sacrifice for our sins. What this Scripture is saying is that God laid it all on the line for us. Knowing that most would reject Him, He made the first move anyway. And He didn't do it with words. He did it with action.

Worldly confidence rests upon things that can be stripped away from us. But through Christ we can be confident that this foundation of love won't be ripped from underneath us whenever we make mistakes. We never earned the love to begin with, so we never have to fear losing it.

GOD'S LOVE—AGAPE LOVE—ISN'T BASED ON HOW GREAT WE ARE. IT'S BASED ON HOW GREAT GOD IS.

It was through His relentless pursuit of us—a pursuit through excruciating self-sacrifice on the cross—that God chose us. His sacrifice is not something that has to be done time and time again. His sacrifice was so pure and potent that it will retain its redeeming power for the rest of eternity.

No longer do we have to strive to find our identity in how well we perform or how perfect we are. We don't have to find our worthiness in our appearance, our abilities, or our social status.

Before we could ever be beautiful, successful, or intriguing …

Before we could ever be sinful, guilty, or broken …

We were pursued by love.

And because God pursued us, we can simply respond. Our acceptance of Christ's sacrifice on the cross is our very acceptance of love itself. When we accept this love, we become God's beloved. The bride of Christ. We don't respond to any other name that He hasn't given us.

Through Christ we will forever be identified by God's love.

TAKE A STAND | IDENTIFY THE LIES

My priority is for you to not only learn these concepts but also apply them. This is what the "Take a Stand" sections are designed for! Take these opportunities to activate the concepts we've explored.

I recommend that you grab a journal or notebook to coincide with your journey through this book. Write down as much as possible! As you work through the writing prompts and prayer points, you'll be able to survey all that God is revealing to you and keep a record of your process as you establish the Four Components of Confidence!

Now that we've explored what it looks like to build your identity based on a framework of lies and we've explored how those lies are introduced, it's time for you to identify the lies you believe so you can uproot them and replace them with a steady foundation of truth.

1. Ask the Holy Spirit

Ask Him to reveal to you the painful events, relationships, or faulty teachings that became open doors for you to receive and believe a lie. Then write them down.

> ‣ Identify these "open door" events.
> ‣ Identify these "open door" relationships.
> ‣ Identify these "open door" teachings (perhaps from culture, family, friends, or church).

2. Identify the Lies

Consider the narratives that shape your view of the world and are not rooted in the truth of God's Word. Then write them down.

> ‣ Identify the lies you believed about yourself.
> ‣ Identify the lies you believed about others.
> ‣ Identify the lies you believed about God.

3. Find Scripture to Counteract the Lies

Read Scripture about who you are in Christ.

> ‣ Some examples include John 1:12; Ephesians 1:7; John 15:16; Colossians 3:1–4; and 2 Corinthians 5:17.

Read Scripture about how you should view others.

▸ Some examples include Ephesians 4:29–32; Luke 6:31; John 15:12; Romans 12:10; and 1 Peter 3:8–12.

Read Scripture about the character of God.

▸ Some examples include 1 John 1:5; 4:8; Hebrews 13:8; 2 Peter 3:9; Isaiah 40:28; and James 1:17.

4. Pray This Prayer

Lord, thank You for revealing to me the open doors that gave way for lies to take root in my mind. I am ready to embrace Your truth.

You showed me that an open door was ___(#1)___, and when that door opened, I believed the lie that ___(#2)___. I denounce these lies because Your Word says ___(#3)___.

Thank You for giving me healing, restoration, and identity through Christ Jesus. I receive Your truth. Empower me to walk in it moving forward.

Repeat this prayer as many times as you need to identify and denounce each lie in your life.

Downplaying My Identity

It was my turn to lead the huddle. My husband and I led the greeting team at our church many years ago. We'd always kick off our Sunday mornings with a little crowd rah-rah. He usually led the group with lots of charisma, zeal, and passion. Our people were known for being the most lively and energetic ones, which always brightened up the volunteers' day. This week was my first time to champion the squad. I didn't take it lightly.

In preparation that week, I read the Bible as I prayed for direction. Tuning my ear to God's heart, I prepped a three-minute message with Scripture and analogies that I believed would perfectly inspire the listeners.

As we circled around each other before church that morning, I was sensitive to how the others would receive me.

Would they prefer to hear Michael?

Would they think of me as worthy to speak into their lives?

Would my ideas resonate with them?

While I was inspiring, I wasn't fully present because I was sinking in insecurity.

As I approached the main part of my message, I prefaced my carefully planned words by saying, "Not to sound extra spiritual, but ..."

While I believed the word God gave me was powerful and pertinent, in that moment I allowed that word to be repressed by my self-preservation.

I didn't want to be seen as self-righteous or holier-than-thou. I also didn't want to stand out as "too much" and become unrelatable or incite jealousy. I wanted to be acceptable and likable to everyone, which was a faulty mentality that led me to dilute my conviction. And … to dilute myself.

Without much thought, I made a few more disqualifying statements throughout my message, and I even purposefully omitted parts of my planned presentation. After all, these volunteers had risen early to drive all the way to serve others; I didn't want anyone to feel like I was wasting their time or making a show.

After I finished, we broke the huddle with a prayer followed by a loud "One, two, three, GO!"

Reflecting on my performance, I felt iffy about my delivery. As I continued to process, a fellow volunteer named Kesha approached. Although she towered over my four-foot-eleven-inch body with her six-foot-two-inch stature, her advance still felt gentle.

I trusted Kesha. Any time we had connected, she was nothing short of warm, genuine, joyful, and confident. She greeted me with a tender smile and made a few seconds of small talk. Then she cut straight to the point.

"I gotta tell you something, Amanda. You don't have to downplay and dismiss your statements. You don't need to say 'not to be too spiritual,' or anything like that. Say what God told you to say. Be confident. Your message was so good. It was worth saying and worth hearing. Please don't feel the need to diminish that."

Her words were refreshing, like a splash of water on my face to wake me up. She was right. Dead right. And I knew it.

The truth was, I had been called by God to give that message. And I wanted to stand tall in its delivery. I longed to have the confidence to speak unapologetically. I craved the conviction to make an impact more than to protect my image.

Yet, even while we were in the context of church, where the expectation is to "be spiritual," I had still dimmed my zeal for God out of my own insecurity.

When called to speak His truth, I sank.

I thanked Kesha for her wise advice and promised to work on this issue. From that moment on, I vowed never to sink beneath my insecurities again.

A False Identity

When we don't know what it means to belong to God, we revert to the elementary ways of calculating our own worth and value. Whenever we don't believe we deserve the abundant life God has given us, then we sink to accept the life we think we do deserve. We bypass the feast on the table that God has prepared for us and settle for the scraps on the floor.

When we choose to accept the false identity of undeserving, unworthy, or insufficient, then we create cycles of defeat and patterns of loss.

If we do not break these false beliefs, then we continue these life-destroying habits. Even worse, these patterns will take root as generational curses that our children will be tasked to break … all because we chose not to believe God has called us to stand in confidence.

Jesus says in John 10:10, "The thief's purpose is to steal and kill and destroy. My purpose is to give them a rich and satisfying life."

Simply put, Jesus died to give us an exceedingly abundant life, and Satan wants to ruin it through lies.

Satan makes us question what God qualified us for, so we play small.

He makes us doubt that righteousness is our inheritance, so we succumb to sin.

He makes us question our significance, so we squander the abundance God sends.

It's a never-ending cycle. Satan's lies sabotage us.

Your True Identity

When you give your life to Christ, you are crucified with Him. From that moment on, it's no longer you who lives, but Christ who lives in you. Once Jesus enters your life, there is no longer any separation between you and Him.

Christ becomes your identifier.

Ephesians 2:13 tells us that, "You have been united with Christ Jesus. Once you were far away from God, but now you have been brought near to him through the blood of Christ."

You're UNITED with Christ.

Imagine being one with The Infinite.

Bonded to Love Incarnate.

"What God has joined together, let no one separate," the Word says in Matthew 19:6 (NIV). If God has put you and Christ together through the power and divine intervention of the Holy Spirit, let no one separate you from Christ … including yourself.

Anything you say about yourself is what you're saying about Jesus.

If you believe you're insufficient, then you're challenging the sufficiency of Jesus.

If you downgrade yourself, then you're downgrading the perfection of Jesus.

If you belittle yourself, then you're belittling the character of Jesus.

Likewise, if you're able to recognize Christ's infinite worth and value independent of any earthly opinions, then you should be able to accept your worth and value too.

In the same way that Christ lives in you:

His holiness lives in you.
His value lives in you.
His grace lives in you.
His truth lives in you.
His love lives in you.

There's another attribute of Christ that people rarely mention, which is the aseity of Christ. His *aseity* simply means that Jesus is self-existent; therefore He is so independent that He does not need anything from us. This idea comes from Acts 17:25, which says, "Human hands can't serve his needs—for he has no needs. He himself gives life and breath to everything, and he satisfies every need."

What if instead of identifying yourself as separate from the aseity of Christ by needing validation from the world, you identified yourself as Christ-existent? As He self-exists, you would Christ-exist, so everything He has, you would claim as your own. You would claim His life, His breath, and His satisfaction as your own.

As you embraced your identity in Christ, you would find that you **gain more** and **need less**.

> You gain belonging in Christ and need less attention from followers.
>
> You gain confirmation in Christ and need less confirmation from people.
>
> You gain more confidence in Christ and need less validation from the world.

REFLECT + PRAY

Reflect

- What are some beliefs you hold about yourself that you don't believe about Jesus? Why?

Pray

- Pray for God to reveal to you any other areas the enemy has infiltrated with false beliefs about yourself.
- Ask God to uproot these false beliefs and to lay a new foundation of your true identity in Him.
- Ask Him to meet you with truth and love in the areas where you've searched for love, acceptance, affirmation, and validation apart from Him.

> # WE'RE NOT CHOSEN BECAUSE OF WHAT WE HAVE DONE. WE'RE CHOSEN BECAUSE OF WHAT *CHRIST* HAS DONE.

The apostle Paul wrote these words to encourage the Ephesian church members to be confident about their identity and inheritance in Christ. Let this prayer remind you of the same:

I pray that from his glorious, unlimited resources he will empower you with inner strength through his Spirit. Then Christ will make his home in your hearts as you trust in him.

Your roots will grow down into God's love and keep you strong. And may you have the power to understand, as all God's people should, how wide, how long, how high, and how deep his love is. May you experience the love of Christ, though it is too great to understand fully. Then you will be made complete with all the fullness of life and power that comes from God.

Now all glory to God, who is able, through his mighty power at work within us, to accomplish infinitely more than we might ask or think. Glory to him in the church and in Christ Jesus through all generations forever and ever! Amen. (Eph. 3:16–21)

TAKE A STAND | EMBRACE THE TRUTH

First,youmustacknowledgethatasachildofGod,youareidentifiedby God—Hislove,Hisgrace,Hislife—andnotbythisworld.Consideringthis, takethefollowingactionitemstorenewyourmindbyembracingthetruth:

1. Write Out a List of Scriptures That Remind You of Your Identity in Christ

Examples:

▸ See how very much our Father loves us, for he calls us his children, and that is what we are! (1 John 3:1)

▸ God raised us up with Christ and seated us with him in the heavenly realms in Christ Jesus, in order that in the coming ages he might show the incomparable riches of his grace, expressed in his kindness to us in Christ Jesus. (Eph. 2:6–7 NIV)

▸ I have been crucified with Christ and I no longer live, but Christ lives in me. The life I now live in the body, I live by faith in the Son of God, who loved me and gave himself for me. (Gal. 2:20 NIV)

2. Create Scripture-Based Affirmations to Speak Aloud over Yourself Every Day

Examples:

▸ My good Father has good intentions for my life. He will never leave me or forsake me.

▸ Nothing will ever separate me from God's love.

› God has given me a plan and a purpose, and I will walk in it.

3. Take the Affirmations a Step Further by Declaring Them in Present Tense

Examples:

› Instead of, "I will be all God has called me to be," say, "I am who God says I am."

› Instead of, "God will get the glory out of my life," say, "God is getting glory out of my story in every season, every day, and every moment."

› Instead of, "I will be confident in God's love for me," say, "I am confident because God loves me."

Chapter 2

DEFINE YOUR DESIGN

Purpose versus Calling

God's divine plan for your life will look different from His plan for others. Your unique path won't parallel that of your best friend, your favorite influencer, or anyone else. You haven't been created to look like anyone else, sound like anyone else, or operate like anyone else.

While every believer carries the same purpose to glorify God, the way God accomplishes that purpose through each person will vary.

Some will glorify God as doctors.

Some will glorify God as missionaries.

Some will glorify God as martyrs.

Nonetheless, all will glorify God distinctly, uniquely, and specifically as He has planned.

Consider one of my favorite analogies that perfectly illustrates this concept.

I want you to imagine you're in the kitchen and you have a scrumptious-looking plate of food. But there's a problem. You need a utensil to eat your food. What utensil are you considering grabbing?

Some people will think of a fork.

Some people will think of a knife.

Some people will think of a spoon.

Now if I told you, "This utensil helps you poke your food, and it has prongs," then you would think of a fork.

If I said, "This utensil helps you cut things," then you would think of a knife.

And if I said, "This utensil helps you scoop liquids," then you would think of a spoon.

This example illustrates the difference between your *purpose* and your *calling*.

The **purpose** for each utensil was the same—to help you eat your food. But the **calling** of each utensil differs. Spoons are called to help you eat foods like cereals and soups, but that's not the same calling that a fork or a knife has. The purpose of the utensils is the same for all, but the callings are different. And the calling of each utensil is determined by its design.

This is the same way it works within the body of Christ. We all share the same purpose—to bring God glory. However, we each have a different calling that we're *designed* to accomplish.

Purpose is the "what."

Calling is the "how."

You won't walk in your calling unless you're aligned with your divine design. Each of us has a responsibility to define how we're individually designed. When you know what God made you for, then you'll align with people, opportunities, and things that position you to do it.

In western Christianity, a lot of believers think that your calling is a path that's already carved out for you and it's your job to find it. But life is funny and unpredictable. Most times, you don't pinpoint your calling; you stumble into it. Something unexpected can expose you to a brand-new world that you become passionate about and master for God's glory.

I never anticipated leaving my world of music to become an author, entrepreneur, or ministry leader. This wasn't my plan for my life. My hopes looked like joining a major symphony as a flutist and advancing in my musical career, teaching private lessons on the side, living a simple and predictable life in the same town, finding a local church, getting married at the age of twenty-five, having kids around twenty-eight, and retiring around sixty.

Instead, I stumbled into YouTubing with Michael and became passionate about sharing the gospel online. Then I married Michael at twenty, finished childbearing by twenty-five, and launched a business and ministry before thirty, all while tackling multiple long-distance relocations.

Like one domino that sparked an unexpected ripple effect, a series of tiny decisions made a lasting impact.

Western Christianity also tends to glorify callings that are more public in nature. While social media would deceive us to believe so, those verified with a blue check mark or those endorsed by a television show don't necessarily carry more verification in the kingdom or endorsement from heaven. Some would say Jesus was "famous" during His time on earth (and for the rest of eternity), but as He hung from the cross, His many followers had dwindled to a faithful few.

Remember, a person's celebrity does not confirm their calling; only Christ does.

Define Your Design

Ephesians 2:10 says, "We are God's masterpiece. He has created us anew in Christ Jesus, so we can do the good things he planned for us long ago."

To accomplish God's plan, you must leverage the talents, opportunities, connections ... and everything else God has given you ... for His glory.

I once read Pastor Rick Warren's book *The Purpose Driven Life*. One chapter helped me clarify my calling with an acronym: SHAPE.[1] So as an ode to that, I've created an acronym that's expanded on the same concept to help you define your DESIGN.

Here's a helpful and memorable tool to empower you to grow confident in your calling using the acronym **DESIGN: Desires, Exposure, Spiritual gifts, Individuality, Genius, Network**.

Let's work through each of the six components.

1. Desires

Your desires are what you care about. They make life meaningful. Not everyone has the same passions, interests, or causes that matter to them. Each person's desires are distinct.

Desires can include:

- ‣ Hobbies, interests, or pursuits you're passionate about
- ‣ Personal goals you want to accomplish

- People, groups, or communities you want to help
- A personal pain point you'd like to help others find freedom from

Some people may care deeply about racial reconciliation, for example. Others may be drawn to helping orphaned children. Some may be advocates for mental health, while others may desire to see more women occupy STEM careers. There is no limit to the ways God can use our passions and desires to accomplish His purpose. The more we align with Christ, the more our desires reflect His.

Our desires shape our decisions, so it's important to acknowledge our desires and discern which ones are worth pursuing.

Imagine you have a friend who desires to move to another country to do missions work and share the gospel and another friend who desires to share the gospel on social media. At face value, you wouldn't be able to decide whether one friend's choice is better than the other's.

While some of our desires are sinful and others are God-given, most desires fall within a gray area. For reasons like these, we've been given the Holy Spirit—He convicts us about which desires to lay down and which to pursue.

God uses desires to shape your destiny. Psalm 37:4 says, "Take delight in the LORD, and he will give you your heart's desires."

Your delight in God's presence will flow through your passions. As you delight yourself in the Lord, He will use your desires to accomplish His purpose through you.

Define Your Desires

A. Make a list of your passions, interests, hobbies, and pursuits.

B. What do you want to accomplish in life? Write that down.

C. What is the wrong in the world that you feel burdened to make right? Write that down.

D. Thank God for the unique desires He's placed within you. Ask Him to align your desires with His heart and to show you which desires to lay down and which to pursue.

2. Exposure

Exposure encompasses everything you've seen, learned, and done. This shapes your unique story.

Your exposure includes:

▸ The positive experiences that have shaped you (successful, enjoyable, etc.)

▸ The negative experiences that have shaped you (traumatic, regretful, painful, etc.)

▸ Your religious, cultural, educational, and economic background

▸ Your ministry, professional, and vocational experiences

▸ Your testimony of how Jesus saved you

Your story—the good, the bad, and the ugly—will all be used for God's glory. Think about it this way: Would you watch a movie about a beautiful woman who graduated from Harvard, landed a successful career, married a handsome entrepreneur, moved to a gorgeous home, and gave birth to three healthy kids who all made straight A's?

Boooooooring!

No one wants to see a movie without a great plot. And do you know what makes a great plot? A massive problem.

The reason we love stories with huge problems and devastating drama is because we find fulfillment watching people face the impossible, find the courage to fight, and then conquer in the end.

YOUR STORY—THE GOOD, THE BAD, AND THE UGLY—WILL ALL BE USED FOR GOD'S GLORY.

You're the main character of your story. Everything you've been exposed to enhances your story and develops your character, equipping you for the victory. Your story is filled with its own ups, downs, twists, and turns … and that's what makes it *juicy*. While your journey likely includes pain, trauma, and regret, it's still a great story. Ultimately, how you conquer challenges is what makes your life worthwhile, especially when you rely on the mighty power of Christ.

Your pain won't have purpose if it's private. You have a story to tell. The more you share your story, the less power it holds over you and the more purposeful your pain becomes. Your "audience" wants to know what the family dynamics in your home were like, what side of town you grew up on, and which giants you had to face to claim your victory.

As you process your life with Christ, God will show you the ways He has pursued you, areas where He protected you, and ways He will prosper you. Rather than despising the pain that has impacted you, embrace how it has made you wiser and shaped your character.

God will use every scene of your story for His glory.

If your story doesn't end with God's glory, then it isn't the end of your story.

Define Your Exposure

A. Describe your religious, cultural, educational, and economic background.

B. Make a list of the top three positive experiences that have shaped your life.

C. Make a list of the top three negative experiences that have shaped your life.

D. Summarize the testimony of how Jesus saved you in three to four sentences. This will help you learn how to share your story and relate to others. Include:
   • What your life was like before Christ
   • The moment you gave your life to Christ and why
   • How your life changed afterward

3. Spiritual Gifts

Your makeup of spiritual gifts is as unique as your fingerprints. You have a certain measure and mix of divine giftings that no one else has. According to 1 Corinthians 12, Romans 12, and 1 Peter 4, we're all given different spiritual gifts, but the same Spirit is the source and distributor of them all.

Spiritual Gifts in the New Testament:

Wise Advice: the ability to give others wise, Spirit-filled advice

Help: the propensity to meet the practical needs of others with a joyful attitude

Leadership: the ability to motivate and equip others to accomplish a purpose

Special Knowledge: the ability to know about a situation supernaturally

Great Faith: a heightened measure of belief in God to do the impossible

Gift of Healing: the ability to restore someone to health

Miracles: the ability to perform signs and wonders that defy the laws of nature

Prophecy: the ability to declare the spoken and written Word of God

Exhortation: the ability to bring out the best in people through encouragement

Giving: a heightened measure of sacrificial giving to meet the material needs of others

Administration: the ability to organize, plan, administer, and lead with excellence

Mercy: a heightened measure of compassion for others in difficult circumstances

Discerning of Spirits: the ability to know which spirit is operating through people and situations and the ability to differentiate the work of God from the work of demons

Tongues: the ability to speak in a never-before-learned language

Interpretation of Tongues: the ability to understand someone speaking in a never-before-learned language[2]

God won't keep you in the dark. It's His will for you to know your spiritual gifts. You will have at least one spiritual gift that you are expected to master and multiply, and you'll likely find that you have more than one.

In addition to the spiritual gifts listed above, some believers are called to hold a "ministry office." Let's take a deeper look at what these roles involve.

Fivefold Ministry Offices:

▸ **Apostle:** Apostles are sent by God on a mission to establish the church by pioneering communities, planting churches, and overseeing leaders. They often appoint, ordain, and oversee leaders. Apostles aren't just gifted people; they're people of integrity.

▸ **Prophet:** A prophet is one who declares the mind and message of God. Prophets are seers and hearers: they will edify and warn the body of Christ on behalf of God. They sometimes predict the future and usually voice God's thoughts in a particular situation. Prophets in the

Bible were not only men; female prophets are listed in the Scriptures as well.

‣ **Teacher:** Teachers are tasked with helping those within the church learn, comprehend, and be transformed by the truth of the Bible. God will judge teachers based on whether they led the flock toward Christ or away from Him by the words they spoke.

‣ **Pastor:** A pastor is raised up by the Lord to care for God's people, as shepherds care for their sheep. Pastoring and teaching often go hand in hand, as the best way to protect and equip the church is through Scripture.

‣ **Evangelist:** While all Christians are called to share the gospel, evangelists make sharing the gospel their vocation and life's mission. Evangelists are commonly missionaries and can be men or women.

Remember, whichever gifts you've been given, they are not given to you to hoard. Rather, your gifts are gifted so you can equip, empower, and edify the church until Christ's return.

Define Your Spiritual Gifts

A. Review the list of spiritual gifts. Ask God to reveal to you which gifts He has given you.

B. Review the fivefold ministry offices. Ask God to reveal to you whether you are called to occupy one of these offices in the body of Christ. (Many believers don't hold fivefold callings, so don't worry if it isn't a part of your unique design.)

C. Whatever He reveals to you, thank God for the gifts He's given you.

D. Make a commitment to steward your gifts well by studying them in Scripture, using them faithfully, and relying on the Spirit's power every step of the way.

4. Individuality

You're not a robot. You're not a clone. You're a human. As a human, you have intrinsic qualities that establish your individuality. God designed every aspect of your existence, and He made no mistake. He intentionally crafted you with your personality, your appearance, and your voice.

Personality

Your personality shapes your you-ness. It is comprised of the mentalities and behaviors that distinguish you from others.

Your mind is the center of every thought you think, emotion you feel, and action you take. A study conducted by researchers from the University of Zurich proved that no two people have the same brain anatomy.[3] Between the influence of our genetics and our experiences, the characteristics of each person's brain are diverse, specific, and individual.

God constructed your brain with intention. Whether you're neurotypical, neurodivergent, right-brained, left-brained, a genius, or anything in between, your unique mind is cherished and esteemed by God. He knows your thoughts before you think them because He was the One who designed them.

Are you introverted or extroverted?

Are you conscientious or whimsical?

Are you creative or pragmatic?

Are you fun-loving or serious?

Are you more rational or emotional?

You could be musically inclined, academically inclined, detail-oriented, or even athletically oriented. The possibilities are endless.

You have personal tendencies, patterns, and preferences that make you one of a kind. Whatever those qualities are, your natural temperaments are critical components to your calling.

Sadly, our God-given personalities are often the very things people try to change or camouflage. While you may feel pressured to become someone you're not, God didn't construct your character to become a copy of someone else.

Your relationship with God isn't one-size-fits-all, either. He craves to connect with you in a way that's authentic to you. Someone else's prayer style, worship style, or Bible study will differ from yours, and that doesn't threaten God. He wired you with that unique individuality in mind.

Therefore, introspection is a worthy investment. Learning more about yourself in order to work on your weaknesses and double down on your strengths will embolden you to stand in confidence.

Appearance

I've never surpassed a height of five feet. For much of my life, I assumed people would "look down" on me and take me less seriously, like a child. I wondered why God had made me so short, so one day, I prayed, "God, why did You make me short?"

He responded clearly, "So that people would be amazed when such great power comes from such a small vessel."

I was comforted to know that my petite frame had been purposefully formed. Since that moment, I've embraced my short stature with confidence rather than feeling insecure because of it. The Bible describes many people whose appearance impacted their calling:

> ‣ Esther's beauty helped her gain the favor she needed with the king to save her people.

> ‣ Samson's long hair and great strength set him apart for a special use.

> ‣ David's age and small stature as a shepherd boy made his victory against Goliath even more astounding.

> ‣ Zacchaeus was very short, which caused him to climb a tree and get Jesus' attention.

> ‣ Jesus was described as having "no beauty that we should desire Him" (Isa. 53:2 NKJV), which prevents us from getting distracted by His appearance so that we can be drawn by His message.

Your appearance is not an accident. God created each person with an image that will make an impact in some way. Your physical differences—such as your skin tone, hair type, eye color, body frame, gender, facial expressions, gestures, and mannerisms—all play a part in your God-given calling.

Voice

The languages you speak, the cadence of your sentences, the tone of your talk, the choice of your words, and every other aspect of your delivery matters to God. Your unique voice carries your perspective, your heart, your culture, and your spirit. Whether your voice is charismatic, spunky, and filled with street slang or composed, refined, and filled with academic jargon, its timbre will resonate with those it is called to reach.

Did you know that Moses was insecure and had a speech impediment? He suffered from a severe stutter, yet despite initial reluctance, he dared to answer God's call and accomplish His purpose. So even if you think you're not well-spoken, God will get the glory out of that too.

Proverbs 18:21 says, "The tongue has the power of life and death" (NIV). The words you speak will manifest either life or death upon this earth. Your voice has the power to either bless or curse. So while your voice is vitally important to your calling, you still must subject it to the power of the Holy Spirit.

WE HAVE THE POWER TO PARTNER WITH GOD TO MANIFEST LIFE AND GRACE ON THE EARTH.

Jesus instructed the disciples to surrender their voices to the Holy Spirit when He said in Mark 13:11, "But when you are arrested and stand trial, don't worry in advance about what to say. Just say what God tells you at that time, for it is not you who will be speaking, but the Holy Spirit." In the same way, we have the power to partner with God to manifest life and grace on the earth.

God placed value in your voice. The more you use it, the more piercing it becomes.

As you speak the Scripture, you will tear down Satan's strongholds. As you preach the gospel, you will build others up in the faith. When you listen first to God, you will speak with supernatural authority. When you let the Spirit speak through you, you'll be unapologetically confident that all of heaven is backing you up.

Your voice is appointed to bless all who hear it. As you're tuned to the intonation of heaven, your voice will resonate with those it's called to reach.

Define Your Individuality

A. Take a personality test such as the Myers-Briggs Type Indicator (MBTI) or the Everything DiSC Application Suite. Write down a list of unique characteristics that define your personality.

B. What special qualities have you been given as part of your appearance? Write those down. Also write down any physical insecurities you have. Ask God for His perspective about your appearance and how He wants to intentionally use it.

C. Ask God what makes your voice unique, how He wants to use it, and who your voice is designed to resonate with. Write down everything He reveals to you.

D. Make a commitment to appreciate your own personality, appearance, and voice and use them for good.

5. Genius

There's a famous quote that says, "Everybody is a genius. But if you judge a fish by its ability to climb a tree, it will live its whole life believing that it is stupid." Following that line of logic, I believe that everyone has been designed with their own form of genius.

Your genius consists of your skills, strengths, and talents. You're endowed with a unique know-how that God expects you to apply and leverage for His glory. This genius need not be compared to that of any other person.

Take a look at the parable of the talents in Matthew 25. Notice that each servant was entrusted with a different portion of silver. The master didn't chastise the servant who'd doubled his bags of silver from two to four even though he didn't earn ten like the first servant. The servants were only judged based on the portion originally given to them, not the amount they were able to generate in return. Likewise, the servant who buried his bag of money was called "wicked and lazy" not because he had been given less than the other servants but because he had done nothing to multiply the little that had been given to him.

The moral of the story is this: don't compare your skills with anyone else's. God holds each of us accountable in accordance with the genius He's placed inside us.

We're responsible for maximizing our own genius for the glory of God. When we stand before God to give an account, no one else will be standing there with us. God won't say, "You multiplied everything I gave you, but you didn't bake as many cakes as Betty Crocker."

Our works won't be evaluated based on what God called someone else to do; they'll only be evaluated based on what God called *us* to do.

Your genius doesn't have to be used in a spiritual context to matter. Colossians 3:23 says, "Work willingly at whatever you do, as though you were working for the Lord rather than for people." God is concerned with the attitude and ethic behind the work you do more than the work itself.

Whether you're skilled at mathematics, you hear perfect pitch, you're competent at budgeting, you're strong in creative thinking, or you're a gifted communicator, God wants to use your genius to glorify Him.

Define Your Genius

A. Create a list of your strengths and talents.

B. Ask God for wisdom on how to multiply the genius He has given you for His glory. Write down anything He reveals to you.

6. Network

God cares about your network. I've heard it said that if God wants to bless you, He will send a person; if Satan wants to curse you, he will send a person.

Proverbs 13:20 says, "Walk with the wise and become wise; associate with fools and get in trouble." Some people call the right relationships "destiny developers" and the wrong relationships "destiny destroyers."

Others say, "We're the sum total of everyone we've ever met."

While hyperbolic, there is some element of truth to this maxim. You will often pick up the qualities and characteristics of those close to you. For this reason, I encourage you to partner with God when picking your people.

God-sent people will complement your design, cultivate your calling, and contribute to your purpose.

Your network consists of your family, friends, faith community, coworkers, mentors, and mentees.

Define Your Network

A. Create a list of every connection in your network. Categorize these connections by the role they play in your life. (For an in-depth way to approach this, see "Categorize Your Connections" in chapter 4.)

B. Ask God for wisdom on how to cultivate your network in such a way that you fulfill His ultimate purpose. ("Cultivate Your Connections" in chapter 4 goes deeper into this.) Write down anything He reveals to you, and commit to being obedient to it.

See Yourself Accurately

You've now defined your unique design so that you can gain clarity. But the ultimate purpose of clarity is to allow you to see yourself accurately so that you can stand confidently in your true identity.

With clarity, your assurance no longer stems from how current you are with trends, how much you're validated by others, or how "in" you are with the cool crowd.

Confidently being who God has called you to be is a simple decision you make every day to …

- **Reject** the notion that you must be like someone else in order to matter.
- **Remind** yourself of who you really are as a beloved child of God.
- **Remain** true to YOU—without compromise.

With clarity, you recognize and embrace the truth:

You're not common. You're not average. You're not ordinary.
You're loved. Valued. Chosen. Called. Gifted. Original.
Equipped. Significant.
No one can replicate you. No one can replace you.
Your perspective carries a heavy weight.
Your voice carries a relevant sound.
Your gifts carry an important mantle.
The world needs you.

When you finally see yourself, you can completely be yourself—without downplaying, belittling, questioning, or wavering. With that clarity, your confidence will come from knowing and being exactly who God called you to be.

Defend Your Design

It's easy to be who God has called us to be when we're in a sheltered circle without many obstacles or challenges in life. However, the real world can be brutal. It's permeated with images and opinions about what we're supposed to believe, what we're supposed to have, and who we're supposed to be.

The world's pervasive suggestion of "not enough" is the driver that compels many people to abandon their true selves and chase after something that appears to offer them more. More significance ... more value ... more worth.

Notice that we're only influenced to believe this when being compared to someone else's standards for us ... not God's. Therefore, the greatest threat to our design is comparison.

Comparison is an opening that exposes us to feelings of inadequacy. If we're not equipped to guard ourselves from external pressures, we'll compromise our originality to find value in conformity.

In the last portion of this chapter, we'll learn the reason we compare, why it hurts us more than it should, and how we can protect ourselves from it. These insights will help us to maintain the purity and integrity of who we're called to be.

The Leaky Roof

A crack in the foundation of a house is only bothersome when it begins to damage other parts of the house. Cracked foundations can cause bricks to break, floors to creak, and roofs to leak.

When the roof leaks, many people will mistakenly assume that the roof is the root of the problem, but the underlying culprit may be a crack in the foundation. In that case, all proposed solutions will mask the symptoms without ever resolving the real problem. If the crack in the foundation isn't addressed, the ceilings will continue to drip.

Comparison is like a leak in the roof. We can try to catch the leaking water with buckets of competition, performance, and perfectionism, but that won't solve the real problem. Every time it rains, we'll just need more buckets.

When we compare ourselves to others, we position ourselves to feel superior or inferior, puffed up or deflated, validated or invalidated, worthy or worthless. Whenever we compare ourselves to others and measure up taller, it's like sunny weather. But whenever we compare ourselves and measure up short, it's like rainfall.

THE GREATEST THREAT TO OUR DESIGN IS COMPARISON.

Everyone will measure up short at some point. A happier, healthier, prettier, wealthier, more talented, and more successful woman will always exist. Measuring up short is an inevitable reality, and it's unavoidable.

Habitually comparing our unfiltered lives with another person's pictures, videos, likes, followers, comments, and shares can cause insecurity to take root. Looking to others as a measuring stick to determine our level of significance is a big problem, especially in today's social media culture, where so much rides on digital engagement and algorithms.

That said, comparison is simply causing the leak in the roof; it's not what's causing the crack in the foundation. Comparison is the secondary issue that's triggered by a much larger, underlying problem—one that can easily be fixed.

The Cracked Foundation

Now that you've defined your design, don't find your worth and value in it. I know it may seem counterintuitive or contradictory, but it's not.

While it's essential for us to function as God created us to, we should never establish our worth in it. This pride in our design will only lead to feelings of superiority or inferiority, neither of which pleases God. We don't want to start believing we're more worthy because of our hair color or more valuable because of our spiritual gifts. We also don't want to place our confidence in who we know, what we can do, or anything else that's subject to change.

Our worth and value are based on our **identity** in Christ—being loved, chosen, and called through Him. This can never be taken away from us. The purpose of defining our design isn't to find our worthiness in it. It's simply to become everything God called us to be while depending on His love, power, and perfection to do it.

The crack in the foundation is caused by believing the lie that "My value is determined by my design, and my worth is determined by my work."

When we believe the lie that our intrinsic design determines our value, we compare our appearance, voice, and experiences with others to draw conclusions about our value. Similarly, when we believe the lie that the quality of our work determines our worth, we will compare our abilities, gifts, and successes with others to measure our worth.

Measuring up short against a standard feels devastating. But what's far more devastating is the belief that measuring up short in one area determines your value and worth.

It causes us to internalize lies like:

"Because I don't meet this beauty standard, I am not valuable."

and

"Because I don't meet this standard of success, I am worthless."

Social media, television, culture … they've all reinforced these lies. We're sent the message that our worth and value are earned when meeting society's standards. We see it everywhere: parents will make their child's grades in school the benchmark for their child's value in the same way that the fashion and beauty industry will evaluate a woman's body and physical appearance to assess her worth.

We fail to recognize that companies are conditioning us to believe we're defective so that we will buy things that can't fix us, accept mentalities that can't liberate us, and follow people that can't lead us.

While societal standards for value and worthiness aren't founded on truth, they're impossible to avoid or ignore. Instead, they keep us standing on an unstable foundation, one that's bound to crack.

Repairing the Cracks

In the same way we seek a professional to help us repair cracks in our home's foundation, we must turn to the one true professional to repair cracks in our spiritual foundation.

You and I aren't the professionals. We're like a homeowner who is ready to get our hands dirty to aid in the repairs. Our therapists can't serve as the "one true" professional either. They're like trained specialists who save us time and energy by giving pointers so we can avoid common mistakes.

You've probably figured where I'm heading with this. The one true professional is Jesus.

In Matthew 7:24–27, Jesus is sitting on a mountain overlooking crowds to teach them about the kingdom of heaven. In one teaching, He illustrates what it's like to build our beliefs upon a solid foundation. In this passage, He says:

> Anyone who listens to my teaching and follows it is wise, like a person who builds a house on solid rock. Though the rain comes in torrents and the floodwaters rise and the winds beat against that house, it won't collapse because it is built on bedrock. But anyone who hears my teaching and doesn't obey it is foolish, like a person who builds a house on sand. When the rains and floods come and the winds beat against that house, it will collapse with a mighty crash.

If the professional is Jesus, then according to this passage, His teachings are the blueprint. Jesus tells the crowds that hearing His teaching isn't what makes us wise builders. The foundation is built when we "follow" His teachings.

How do we do this?

First, note that the word *follow* is not included in the original text of this verse. The original word is transliterated by *Strong's Concordance* as *poieó,* which means to "make or do."[4]

Here's where it gets interesting …

The usage of the word *poieó* is notated as "make, manufacture, construct" and "do, act, cause." Jesus used actionable steps such as *construct, make, do, act,* and *cause.* This is because our beliefs are expressed, completed, and proven as we construct, make, do, act, and cause.

Simultaneously, as we behave in accordance with our beliefs, we become wise. This wisdom not only acknowledges the truth that Jesus taught but also enables us to construct our lives upon the solid foundation of His truth, causing the truth to manifest in our lives.

As we believe in God and trust in His plan by embracing our identity and defining our design, He will repair every crack of lies until we're firmly planted upon His truth.

TAKE A STAND | REPAIR THE CRACKS

Let's consider how professionals repair cracked foundations.

First, they excavate a trench to expose the foundation.

Then, they replace any damaged cement.

Lastly, they seal any cracks with special cement.

You will approach repairing the cracks in your foundation the same way.

1. Expose the False Beliefs

What aspects of your design do you measure or compare with others to determine your worth and/or value? Write these down.

Where did each false belief come from? Write it down.

Acknowledge and write down reasons why these beliefs are false.

2. Replace Damaged Beliefs with the Truth

Verbally come out of agreement with these false beliefs through Jesus.

Example:

"I denounce the belief that my worth and value are determined by my appearance. I uproot this lie from my mind and cancel its effects in my life by the power and authority of the blood of Jesus."

Verbally come into agreement with the truth using Scripture.

Example:

▸ *I declare that* "I am fearfully and wonderfully made." (Ps. 139:14 NIV)

▸ *I declare that I am made* "in the image of God." (Gen. 1:27)

▸ *I declare that I belong to* "a chosen race, a royal priesthood, a holy nation, a people for [God's] own possession." (1 Pet. 2:9 ESV)

▸ Therefore, I know that my value is proven in being a child of God. I am worthy not because of what I have done, but because of what God has done.

3. Seal Cracks of Doubt with Action

Commit to behaving in alignment with the truth.

▸ When you're tempted to reject your identity to seek worth and value from the world, speak Scriptures to remember who God created you to be.

▸ When you're tempted to compare yourself to others, thank God for the way He uniquely formed you.

▸ When insecurities arise, remind yourself that your identity rests in the finished work of Jesus.

Connection

COMPONENT OF CONFIDENCE #2

The Importance of Connection

Now that we've developed **clarity** about who you are in Christ, let's explore the second component of confidence: **connection**. This component is all about who you're living life with.

Who you're connected to will not only configure your confidence but will also determine your destiny. Therefore, the next two chapters will examine how you:

- ▸ **Connect with God** | Hear God's Voice
- ▸ **Connect with Others** | Pick Your People

You may have heard it said, "While you can't change the people around you, you can *choose* the people around you." And that particular choice is a very important one. If you choose wisely, you'll find real riches in your relationships and real purpose tied to the people in your life.

As you connect with God intimately and connect with others intentionally, you'll establish the network you need to support you, allowing you to remain confident through the storms of life.

Chapter 3

CONNECT WITH GOD

Connected to the Source

Imagine there's a straight line descending from heaven that hovers right above dry land. This line radiates a glorious white light, making it impossible to miss. Gradually lifting your chin, your eyes venture to find where the line begins, but the light pierces through the clouds, extending higher than the tallest building.

Fascinated, you jog toward the light. The closer you get, the more peace you feel. The comforting warmth assures you that you're moving in the right direction.

When you arrive, you reach your hand up to the beam. As it contacts your hand, nothing happens. It seems safe. So without hesitation, you step directly underneath the line. Instantly, power surges from the crown of your head to the soles of your feet. You feel fully invigorated by the force while also feeling lighter and more buoyant because of it.

In a moment, everything makes sense. You're present. You're lucid. You're clear. You're exactly where you're supposed to be—in **connection with the divine**.

Now the line of light travels with you, empowering you everywhere you go. In connection, miracles materialize everywhere. You bless everyone you encounter. Your gifts are maximized, enabling you to make the most out of every opportunity. You know which doors are safe and which are traps.

Every doubt you ever had is erased, and every truth becomes incontestable. So, with great authority, you declare what is true. Without apology, you dismantle what is false. You know what you're supposed to do, who you're supposed to meet, and how you're supposed to think. You're walking in line with your destiny.

In connection with the source, you've found your spiritual confidence.

This example is an illustration of your connection with God. Your level of connection with the God of heaven will determine your level of spiritual confidence on earth.

Spiritual Confidence

Plenty of experts teach strategies to become confident in our bodies, confident in dating, confident in professional environments, confident in social settings, and more. However, few people teach us how to become spiritually confident. Since our culture is enamored with what we can see with our own eyes, we underestimate the impact that spiritual confidence will make.

Spiritual confidence changes EVERYTHING.

Those who are spiritually confident are often referred to as "anointed" or "powerful" because of the authority and influence they carry. While many assume this influence comes from a higher degree of spiritual verification, the real thing only comes through a deeper degree of **spiritual connection**.

Sometimes we rely too heavily on spiritual leaders, especially when we assume a pastor, teacher, or prophet is far above our realm of giftedness, favor, or **closeness to God**. If we become infatuated with their anointing, we can become disinterested in cultivating our own.

Insecurity can also plague us when we spend time alone with God. We may find ourselves wondering:

Is this God speaking, or is this me?

Am I reading this verse right?

Should I be feeling God's presence right now?

This happens because we've relied so heavily on other people's connections with God that we distrust our *own* connection with God. However, when Jesus died on the cross, the veil—the barrier that once separated us from firsthand access to God—was torn. Christ's sacrifice granted us direct access to connect with God for ourselves.

Jesus says it Himself in John 15:5–8:

Yes, I am the vine; you are the branches. Those who remain in me, and I in them, will produce much fruit. For apart from me you can do nothing. Anyone who does not remain in me is thrown away like a useless branch and withers. Such branches are gathered into a pile to be burned. But if you remain in me and my words remain in you, you may ask for anything you want, and it will be granted! When you produce much fruit, you are my true disciples. This brings great glory to my Father.

This passage shows that our connection with Christ will determine whether what we do on earth will have any lasting value. Whatever we accomplish without Christ is forever useless, but whatever we accomplish with Christ is eternally meaningful.

Simply put, our partnership with heaven will affect our purpose on earth.

We can't produce anything *for* God *without* a direct connection with God. The more we partner, the more we produce. So as we partner *with* God, we produce the best work *for* God.

REFLECT + PRAY

Reflect

- What factors discourage you from connecting with God? Why?
- What factors encourage you to connect with God? Why?
- In what ways can you minimize what discourages you from connecting with God and maximize what encourages you to connect with Him?

Pray

Lord, thank You that I have firsthand access to Your presence and power. Please give me a greater desire to connect with You, and help me to partner with You in all things.

Spiritual Insecurity

During a certain time in my life, I became spiritually insecure because of the people I saw around me. If their convictions were more rigid than mine and if they presented themselves as hyper-spiritual, I would assume they were closer to God than I was.

These same people devised accusations disguised as prophetic words to tell me that I was secretly living in sin, possessed by an unholy spirit, and operating with ill intent. While their words were far from true, their judgments devastated me.

OUR PARTNERSHIP WITH HEAVEN WILL AFFECT OUR PURPOSE ON EARTH.

Since my security in my own relationship with God had eroded with time, I would question myself whenever their "prophecies" didn't align with what I knew God was showing me. In this process, I began doubting my own encounters with God, questioning if I had really experienced that spiritual encounter or if it was simply a mirage.

In the thick of my spiraling, wondering if I needed another round of repentance, another session of deliverance, or another self-assessment, God sent me a real prophet. Her name was Tiphani.

At one of my lowest points, Tiphani knocked sense into me like a coach getting a player's head right for the game-winning shot. With great authority, she told me that the reason I was going through this pain was not because I was some hellion or Jezebel who didn't truly love Jesus; the real reason I was in so much despair was because I was trusting the voices around me more than I was trusting the voice of God.

She told me two important things I'll never forget. The first was this: "Your love for people clouds your discernment about them."

With those few words, she helped me to recognize that I was blinded by believing the best about those who'd already shown me who they were. The truth that Christians had the desire to deceive and manipulate through spiritual language and Scripture was a hard pill for me to swallow. But when I finally accepted that truth, I was able to see both them and God clearly.

Then Tiphani left me with this: "Amanda, you need to PLEAD to God. Literally BEG God to break the opinions of people off of you." She said this on the verge of shouting.

And you know what? Tiphani was right. She had given me the gospel truth. I had allowed myself to be tossed to and fro by every little opinion that a Bible-touting person had spoken of me. Gaslighted by what others were saying about me, I had begun to question the voice of God.

Like a player in the game, I decided to follow the coach's advice. I didn't just pray; I pleaded. Each day my aching soul wrestled with God. I struggled to believe that I was chosen, appointed, loved, cherished, considered, seen, and favored by Him.

With an exhausted body, I fasted.

With a weary soul, I wept.

With a shaking voice, I worshipped.

With a desperate heart, I begged.

Through it all, God was faithful. With my complete dependency on His chain-breaking power, He shattered the shackles that had constrained me to the idolatry of people. When I glorified God's Word above every other word spoken by man, the idol of people came crashing down. When the false idol stopped blocking my view, I could finally see God's truth clearly. I could see Him for who He was, and I could see myself in relation to Him.

He was holy, pure, righteous, faithful, and kind.

I was His beloved daughter—redeemed, cherished, accepted, purified, and sanctified.

I COULD SEE HIM FOR WHO HE WAS, AND I COULD SEE MYSELF IN RELATION TO HIM.

Now, I want you to hear God's voice for yourself too. Sharpening your ability to hear God's voice will give you a confidence that can't be taken away from you, no matter how many other opinions come your way.

In this chapter we'll challenge the temptation to rely on the voices of people and learn how to hear God's voice for ourselves.

This Isn't New

This propensity to trust in people more than God isn't new to our generation. Even the apostle Paul corrected the Corinthian church in 1 Corinthians 3 because they were bragging about following certain human leaders. With great conviction, Paul rebuked:

> When one of you says, "I am a follower of Paul," and another says, "I follow Apollos," aren't you acting just like people of the world?
>
> After all, who is Apollos? Who is Paul?...
>
> So don't boast about following a particular human leader. For everything belongs to you—whether Paul or Apollos or Peter, or the world, or life and death, or the present and the future. **Everything belongs to you**, and you belong to Christ, and Christ belongs to God. (vv. 4–5, 21–23)

Paul was addressing the church's spiritual immaturity. He warned the people of the church not to elevate the messenger because the power is in the message. To shift their narrow perspective, Paul concluded, "Everything belongs to you."

What a striking statement. The phrase *everything belongs to you* is translated in some Bible versions as "All things are yours." Can you fathom that through Christ, **all things** are already yours?

John Piper, founder of desiringGod.org and chancellor of Bethlehem College and Seminary, wrote a stunning commencement speech on the concept "all things are yours." In it he says,

When a sense of insecurity in your abilities, in your job, in your ministry, in your theology, tempts you to attach yourself to someone stronger, someone more competent, more esteemed, more gifted, more secure, don't do it. You don't need to do it because **all things are yours.**...

When the craving for secondhand significance and worth and power and authority tempt you to grasp for it vicariously by boasting in men, don't do it. You don't need to do it because **all things are yours.**[1] [emphasis added]

Are you comprehending this truth bomb?

You aren't more established because you're led or endorsed by a big name. You're already backed by the Name Above All Names! You don't need to seek out a "covering" to find comfort in a false sense of credibility. You're already covered by God.

His Spirit is your credential. **You** are God's anointed! **You** are God's chosen! **You** are God's favored! **All things are yours!**

Spiritual confidence comes when you know that everything already belongs to you. Be confident that in Christ you have perfect shalom—nothing broken, nothing missing. You're already loved. You're already equipped. God has already blessed you with every spiritual blessing in the heavenly realms.

Most importantly, you have direct access to your heavenly Father. When He was crucified, Jesus tore the veil between you and the Father through His sacrifice. Then He sent us the Holy Spirit, who speaks to us and through us. We are now able to communicate directly with the Father through the power of the Holy Spirit who lives in each of us.

REFLECT + PRAY

Reflect

- What contributes most to your own spiritual insecurity?
- What are some blessings God has given you through Christ that can be used to combat those insecurities?

Pray

Lord, help me to recognize that You've already given me everything and that I can have complete access to You. Help me to hear Your voice and follow it with confidence.

Hearing God's Voice

God doesn't have a speaking problem; we have a listening problem. Listening to God is impossible when His voice is drowned out by the opinions of people. Hearing God's voice requires us to turn down the noise so we can:

- Learn God's voice
- Create a lifestyle of listening to His voice
- Sharpen our ability to discern God's voice from other voices

When we are competent in doing these three things, we're able to operate with spiritual confidence. Let's explore hearing God's voice, and then we'll practice applying this concept in our daily lives.

God Has Already Spoken

The first concept we need to understand is that God has ALREADY spoken. The Bible is the written Word of God, given for our benefit. We won't know the voice of God if we don't read the Word of God. This is because God's voice will *never* contradict God's Word.

There's a popular adage that goes, "Don't say God is silent when your Bible is closed." *Cheeky and true.*

While all other books can offer trending opinions and temporary knowledge, the Word of God tells eternal *truth*. It is powerful and effective, standing the test of time. The Word was with God in the beginning, and when all the world fades away, the Word will be there in the end.

While all other books are inanimate, the Word of God is alive.

So often, we search for a sign from heaven or a word from a prophet when the very answers we seek are right there waiting for us in Scripture. And would God have it any other way? The truth is that God wouldn't want us dependent on any voice that doesn't require us to read His Word.

WE WON'T KNOW THE VOICE OF GOD IF WE DON'T READ THE WORD OF GOD.

Another reason we may not search the Scriptures is because we don't know how to approach the Scriptures.

John 1:1 says, "In the beginning was the Word, and the Word was with God, and the Word was God" (NIV).

This verse is referring to Jesus Himself as "the Word." John is illustrating the eternal truth that Jesus and His Word are inseparable. He inspired the Scripture through His Spirit, then the Scriptures prophesied about Him, and then He fulfilled the prophecies. All Scripture points to Jesus.

If we want to approach Jesus, then we must approach the Scripture. And when we approach the Scripture, we must approach it to find Jesus—not ourselves.

The Bible isn't about us; it's about Christ. If we approach the Scriptures to find ourselves, it leads to misinterpretation and misapplication. But when we approach the Scriptures to find Jesus, we find both Jesus and ourselves.

Hebrews 4:12 says, "The word of God is alive and active. Sharper than any double-edged sword, it penetrates even to dividing soul and spirit, joints and marrow; it judges the thoughts and attitudes of the heart" (NIV).

With every other book we have the power to judge, but the Bible is the only book with the power to judge us.

While we may not understand every passage, every historical nuance, or even every biblical name, we must keep reading. Even when it feels as if the Word is disrupting our comfort, we must continue to dig. The more we seek, the more we find. The more questions we ask, the more answers we get.

As we read the Bible, we must filter our experiences through the Bible—not filter the Bible through our experiences. Our emotions and experiences can't bring us life or freedom. Only the truth can do that. So we can't expect to read the Bible and agree with or enjoy every verse. If the Bible always fits within the narrow framework of our western worldview in the twenty-first century, could we legitimately trust it to be true?

We should never filter the Bible; the Bible should filter us.

Greater Access

Many times, we think that God spoke more clearly to the people in the Old Testament. We read that God appeared to Abraham in the form of a man, God led Moses with the glory cloud, and God spoke to Sarah through angels.

We assume they had greater access to God, but the truth is they had LESS access to God. Through the sacrifice Jesus made on the cross, we have been given FULL access to approach the Father. Not only that, but we now have the New Testament to guide us.

In John 14:12, Jesus says, "Very truly I tell you, whoever believes in me will do the works I have been doing, and they will do even greater things than these, because I am going to the Father" (NIV).

In this passage, Jesus was depicting the gift that all previous generations coveted—His very own presence. The Holy Spirit lives inside us, teaches us, and convicts us. He is the One who helps us to interpret the written Word of God and hear the spoken word of God.

Because of this, we no longer need burning bushes, angelic visitations, or glory clouds to hear God's voice. The Holy Spirit writes God's Word on our hearts. Our spiritual maturity isn't evidenced in how many hyperspiritual encounters we have. It's evidenced in our ability to hear God without needing these kinds of supernatural encounters.

God's presence, power, and perspective are available to us now more than ever, but it's our responsibility to access them.

Make the Connection

Think about it this way. If we want to turn on a light, we must have THREE things: **power**, **provision**, and a **point of contact**.

Have you ever paid your light bill on time but then a thunderstorm caused you to lose power?

This is what it looks like when you have **provision** but no **power**. It's not that the power company is withholding electricity from you. Power is still available from the source. But when your environment blocks you from accessing that power source, you can't tap into the provision you are entitled to.

What does it look like, though, when you have **power** but no **provision**?

Let's say you just moved into a new home but it's taking you longer than you anticipated to get energy connected to your new address. While the home is purposed for power, you have no electricity provider. No provider. No provision.

But let's not forget ... To turn on the lights, there's a necessary third element, which is a **point of contact**. You can have power and provision, but if you never touch the light switch to make the point of contact, you'll never access the power and provision that are yours for the taking.

Now let's shift this example from the physical to the spiritual realm.

God is our spiritual **provider**. He provides for our every need and has the **power** to deliver His provision. But why is it that we so rarely acknowledge His power in our lives?

Here's the reason: there is no **point of contact**.

So what is the point of contact that allows us to access God's power and provision? What is the "light switch" that gives us access to the provision that He's offering us?

PRAYER.

Many times, when there is an absence of power and/or provision in our lives, there is also an absence of prayer. We're not flipping the light switch to receive all He has to give us!

Prayer is the point of contact that gives us access to God's power and provision.

There's no need that God can't meet. God has the power to provide for our pressing material needs *and* our buried intangible needs. And the deepest need we have that only God can meet is the need for His presence. Prayer not only empowers us to see God's hand move for us, but it also enables us to feel God's presence move within us. It also opens our hearts so that we can hear God's voice speak to us.

REFLECT + PRAY

Reflect

- What does your current commitment to prayer reveal about your connection to God?
- What distractions or obligations drown out your prayer life?
- How can you use prayer as a regular point of contact with God?

Pray

- Thank God for the opportunity to approach Him in prayer at all times.
- Praise God for the times He has answered your prayers and met your needs.
- Ask God to help you be sensitive to His voice and prompting.

Listening for Intimacy

The primary goal of prayer isn't instruction—it's intimacy.

When we approach God for instruction but not for intimacy, He may seem silent. This is because when we work for God more than we sit with God, we miss Him.

While it's easy to work for God without being close to God, He is more concerned with us giving Him access to our hearts than giving Him the work of our hands. God knows that if He has our hearts, then our hands will follow.

Think about it.

Would God want us to forego His presence to attain something He has already promised?

Would a loving father want his daughter to serve him without ever spending time with him?

Of course not.

God wants our hearts, and our spirits crave His. The more we know God's heart, the easier it is to understand His will. It's within intimacy **with God** that we find instruction **from God**.

Now, reading the Bible isn't equated to intimacy with God.

In John 5, when Jesus was rebuking the Jewish leaders, He said,

> And I assure you that the time is coming, indeed it's here now, when the dead will hear my voice—the voice of the Son of God. And those who listen will live…. (v. 25 NLT)
>
> You search the Scriptures because you think that in them you have eternal life; and it is they that bear witness about me, yet you refuse to come to me that you may have life. (vv. 39–40 ESV)

Jesus made it plain: learning about God isn't the same as listening to God. Reading the Bible is essential, but it's incomplete. We can explain God through Scripture, but we experience Him through prayer.

Prayer isn't just our opportunity to make our requests known to God. It's also God's opportunity to make His heart known to us. God desires intimacy with us, and intimacy can only come with reciprocity.

Those with the most intimate connection with God understand that prayer isn't just about us speaking, but it's also about us **listening**. The more intently we **listen** to His heart, the more intentionally we can follow His will.

Prayer in Practice

Years ago, Michael took his first spiritual retreat to be alone with God. He checked into a nearby monastery led by Christian monks. When I dropped him off, the place was immersed in tranquility and restfulness. While at the monastery, Michael took a class that taught him how to pray. In the teaching, the instructor taught about the concept of the Four Stages of Prayer found in a book they recommended.[2]

The Four Stages of Prayer

1

Talking at God:
Like a child who has memorized their mealtime and bedtime prayers, we approach God in a way that is rehearsed and scripted. Prayer is performative.

2

Talking to God:
When we talk to God, we are open and vulnerable about our needs and requests. We may even be skilled at thanking and praising Him. But it ends there. We talk to God but leave no space for Him to respond.

3

Listening to God:
Not only do we talk to God genuinely, but we lean in for His response. We give Him room to communicate with us, comfort us, challenge us, and change us. We build a true two-way relationship with Him.

4

Being with God:
This is a contemplative state of prayer of neither speaking nor listening. Like a newborn child nursing at its mother's breast, we calmly trust that God expects nothing more from us than to rest in His arms and receive His love. This requires no words; it simply requires a time, a place, and an intention to acknowledge and experience His presence.

Looking at this list, which stage of prayer would you put yourself in? What is your goal and agenda with prayer?

Many find themselves in stage one and two of prayer, which is why they lack spiritual confidence. As we mature in Christ, the majority of our prayer time should be spent in stages three and four—*listening* to God and *being* with God.

When I shifted my approach to prayer, I first had to release my expectations about what prayer was supposed to be. It became less about me changing God's mind and more about me accepting God's heart. At first, it seemed awkward to sit in silence, but that very silence enabled me to hear His voice more clearly.

The Still, Small Voice

God speaks to us in many ways.

Through His Word.
Through other people.
Through signs and wonders.
Some have heard God audibly.
Some hear God through dreams and visions.
Some have heard God through angelic visitations.

But there is one way God speaks that is depicted in the story of Elijah. First Kings 19:11–13 says,

The LORD said to Elijah, "Go, stand in front of me on the mountain, and I will pass by you." Then a very strong wind blew until it caused the mountains to fall apart and large rocks to break in front of the LORD. **But the LORD was not in the wind.** After the wind, there was an earthquake, **but the LORD was not in the earthquake.** After the earthquake, there was a fire, **but the LORD was not in the fire.** After the fire, there was a quiet, gentle sound [a still, small voice]. When Elijah heard it, he covered his face with his coat and went out and stood at the entrance to the cave. (NCV)

Sometimes, we want God to speak LOUD and "big." We plead, "GOD GIVE ME A SIGN!" But in this scenario with Elijah, we see that God wasn't in the earthquake, God wasn't in the fire, and God wasn't even in the wind. He was in the whisper … a gentle, still, small voice.

God still speaks through a "still small voice" (KJV) today through His *rhema* word.

In the Bible, there are two different Greek words used to refer to the Word of God, both of which can be found within *Thayer's Greek Lexicon*. The first is *logos*—commonly known as the unchangeable written Word of God, which is Scripture.[3] The second is *rhema*—the right-now, on-time voice of God that leads us in our everyday decisions.[4] This voice is alive and always speaking. We need *both* the *logos* and *rhema* to connect with God.

A *rhema* word can come as a prophetic word from someone. It can even be an unexplainable "knowing" or understanding of God's heart. It can also be a sense of distinction between right and wrong. If you grew up in church, you may even call it a "check within your spirit."

This can be that "red light" or "green light" feeling or a thought that falls in line with some of the following statements:

Red light:
"I wouldn't do that if I were you."
"I know you think it's a good thing, but it's not a good thing."
"Slow down."
"Pause."

Green light:
"It's time to end the secret."
"It's time to take the next step."
"Everyone is going left, but ... go right."

God's position determines His perspective. Because the Father sees, knows, and hears what we cannot from His position in heaven, the Holy Spirit gives us His instruction so that we aren't led astray by following our earthly assumptions.

Did you know that in Acts 16:6–7, the Holy Spirit prevented Paul and Silas from preaching the word in the province of Asia and the province of Bithynia? Can you believe that? You'd think that because they're spreading the gospel, they should spread it everywhere, sparing no place. But it was Paul and Silas's sensitivity to God's *rhema* word that kept them safe.

I've heard it said that no one who is intimate with God will ever be intimidated by people. I couldn't agree more. In my many years of listening to God, I've found that the more I obey the still, small voice inside me, the more I see God's power working through me.

TAKE A STAND | HEAR GOD'S VOICE

1. Learn God's Voice

▸ Compose a list of Scriptures that describe God's character and voice.

▸ Then write down a list of fifteen to twenty characteristics that define His voice.

▸ Lastly, pray to ask God to help you hear, trust, and follow His voice.

2. Listen to God's Voice

▸ Envision Jesus standing in front of you.

▸ Next, ask Jesus a question you'd like to know the answer to. (Example: "Father, can You show me why I'm struggling to let go?")

▸ Then leave space and silence for Jesus to answer.

▸ Write down whatever you think, feel, notice, sense, imagine, envision, remember, and more. God may bring related Scripture to mind. Other times, He may give you a knowing of what is true. Many times, God will guide your thoughts and open your eyes to the truth.

3. Discern God's Voice

It's good to recognize the characteristics that highlight the differences between God's voice, Satan's voice, and the voice of our flesh. Reference the Voices Chart below the next time you're struggling to discern between voices. To strengthen your own discernment, **personalize this chart for each voice in your own journal or notebook**. The more skilled you become at discerning the source of a voice on your own, the more confident you'll be in following God's voice.

Voices Chart

Voice of the Lord	Voice of the Enemy	Voice of the Flesh
Motivated by love	Motivated by hate	Motivated by desire
Says what is true	Says what is false	Says what is convenient
Strengthens your spirit	Weakens your spirit	Strengthens your flesh
Voice of conviction	Voice of condemnation	Is not convicted by sin
Faith, hope, and love	Steal, kill, and destroy	Lust of the flesh, lust of the eyes, and the pride of life
Breeds hope	Breeds despair	Breeds desire
Brings clarity	Brings confusion	Uses human reasoning
Fulfills God's will	Fulfills Satan's will	Fulfills self-will
Protects you and others	Exploits you and others	Preserves self at the expense of others

Chapter 4

CONNECT WITH OTHERS

Soft Front, Strong Back

I once had a DM conversation with Amy, an old classmate, about her spiritual beliefs. Amy knew I was a Christian, and I knew she ascribed to other beliefs. Curious about her take on current events from her worldview, I continued asking questions and learning more. Over the course of weeks, we enjoyed learning about one another's perspective of life.

After much rich conversation, Amy gave me one of the most uniquely validating compliments I've ever received.

She said, "You're humble, open, and approachable while also strong in your beliefs. Brené Brown calls it having a *soft front* and a *strong back*.[1] It's a good indicator of who's done the work and who's all talk."

Those words stuck with me. *I hadn't always been this way.*

I remember the painful years when I was hungry for validation, sensitive to criticism, nervous about social interaction, and feeling like I didn't belong. For so long I lacked the social skills and the confidence to make others feel this welcomed in my presence. Amy's words validated all the inner work I had done to become the woman I'd always wanted to be.

What she said resonated with me for another reason too. The nature of the woman Amy was describing—having a "soft front" and a "strong back"—is exactly how confident women should relate to others.

When a woman has rooted her confidence in Christ, it is felt by everyone around her. This woman is receptive toward everyone while remaining resolute in her values. Confident women won't feel the need to be harsh, dismissive, or callous toward anyone. They've done the inner work needed to lay their egos down and show love toward others, whether they agree with them or not.

This is why confident women attract and form quality connections: they're generous with their love yet selective with their relationships.

Their posture of humility, openness, and sincerity is esteemed by those who possess the same qualities. While their demeanor draws in many, confident women will only surround themselves with a choice company of people—those who draw them closer to Christ, those who align with their values, and those who are trustworthy and safe.

This is the appeal we're called to exude as women of God.

We don't have to do much to accomplish this. This is simply the result of an embraced identity in Christ. We know who we are, we know what we believe, and we know what we want.

With a soft front and a strong back, it's not hard to attract the healthy, secure connections we all long for. And since our values will already be firmly established, it's also not hard for us to recognize those who align with them too.

What *will* require more effort from us is addressing any existing connections in our lives that **don't** align with our values. That *don't* push us closer to Jesus. That *don't* feel quite safe.

What do we do with those?

We either establish new parameters around such relationships or we remove them altogether. Doing so affords us healthier experiences and continued growth. **This** is the inner work we do in preparation for the secure connections that will come our way.

I'll share a peek into the journey of my own inner work that took me from an insecure woman who formed insecure connections to a confident woman who established secure connections—and how you can do the same too.

Craving Connection

I always felt different.

Maybe it was the result of being the unlikely offspring of a white woman raised on a farm in a small town in Minnesota and a Spanish-speaking black man who had immigrated from the Dominican Republic. Being an entire school year ahead for my age while never surpassing four feet eleven inches in height could also have been a factor. I also had a natural bent toward sensitivity and creative expression through the arts, poetry, and music, so let's not rule that possibility out.

Most likely, I'm sure it was somehow attributed to being saved before the age of six and walking with the conviction of the Holy Spirit before I could fully comprehend it. For whatever reason, much of my life was spent feeling like a foreigner.

Throughout middle and high school, I struggled to make and keep friends with girls. Feeling socially awkward, I never seemed to have the right words to say.

How do people make friends?

Who do I sit by in the cafeteria?

Should I just pull up a chair around someone and strike up a conversation?

Are we supposed to talk about boys?

What if I don't know the latest dances?

I craved feminine connection and genuine friendship, but it seemed like I was invisible. So I hung with the guys, ate lunch in the band hall, and kept myself busy.

Then I arrived at Southern Methodist University in Dallas, Texas, at the ripe old age of seventeen.

While my high school campus had been located in a low-income, high-crime area, my college campus was central to the neighborhood of the top 1 percent. Some people referred to the campus as "Southern *Millionaires* University" for obvious reasons. The picturesque campus was brimming with tanned and toned blonde-hair, blue-eyed girls driving the newest Porsches with Starbucks in hand. It was flooded with Zachs and Chads decked out in sunglasses, backward baseball hats, boat shoes, and pastel Polo shirts. I was one of the few specks of pepper in a great big sea of salt.

Culture shock, to say the least.

I wasn't that hot college girl with designer bags and expensive hobbies. I was the flute girl attending on a music scholarship (plus the extra help of a diversity initiative), who had working-class parents and relied on public transportation.

Within the first few weeks, I didn't find my friend clique as many of the other freshmen had. Tied down by my long-distance boyfriend, I spent a lot of time chatting with him on my computer in my dorm, watching my roommate and other students go out and have the time of their lives.

I felt like the oddball. I just didn't fit.

As time passed, I built friendships with guys on campus and had a few friendly acquaintances I could sit next to in the cafeteria, but I still craved deeper connection.

Seeking Connection

As the spring semester of sophomore year progressed, I wanted to expand my social horizon even more. Even after Michael and I started dating, I knew I couldn't just be Michael's girlfriend. I needed friends. So I decided I would join a multicultural sorority.

The rushing process of joining a sorority was invigorating. For the first time, it seemed as if girls wanted me around. I found it significantly easier to show up for rush events than to strike up a conversation with a random girl in the cafeteria. The interviews and service functions felt like an audition, and with my music background, I knew how to audition. Performing was a breeze.

I went through the recruitment process throughout the spring semester and crossed toward the end with a grand step-show-routine probate and reveal. It felt like a long-awaited dream. For once in my life, I had a group of girls I could call my own. We scheduled brunches and outings, and we created exclusive hand signs and signature strolls, all while wearing matching paraphernalia with Greek letters that represented my belonging. I connected with other fraternities and sororities by virtue, making me more visible on campus than ever before.

I finally felt validated as a college girl. I had already landed the guy of my dreams. And now this! Finding lifelong girlfriends is what every college story should entail … right?

Despite achieving all those goals, I still felt out of place in the sorority. I ignored the feeling for many months, assuming that my connections would deepen with time. However, my concerns were rooted more deeply than that.

One night, one of my sisters admitted that she didn't invite me into as many conversations and outings as the other girls because she didn't feel compatible with me. Another shared that she'd anticipated we'd grow closer and was disappointed when we didn't. I'd had no idea.

There was another situation with one of my sisters that arose that I should have handled a lot differently. Word spread quickly about my approach. While I became aware of my wrongs and apologized for the missteps I took once I was confronted, it was too late. This had already led to harsh gossip, undue rumors, and false accusations within the group. It wounded me deeply.

From then on, the more I attempted to connect, the more they seemed to push me away. With the exception of a few, I felt mischaracterized and judged.

While the disappointment of feeling misunderstood weighed on me, deep down I had already known that something was *off.* I had been feeling it all along, but the disapproval of the group was what gave me a sobering reality check.

The time had come for me to be honest with myself—the organization was never aligned with my identity or destiny. I was trying too hard to be liked, validated, understood, and accepted by people who weren't headed in the same direction as me.

The Courage to Leave

There have been several times in my life when I've had to muster enough courage to leave relationships and environments knowing that I'd be disliked because of it. Leaving this sorority was one of them.

After weeks in prayer and deliberation, I was deeply convicted that my time as a Greek should end. I denounced the sorority, turned in all my paraphernalia, and left the group chats. My relationships with my previous sisters fizzled out just as fast. In the process, something broke off of me.

As soon as I freed myself from those obligations, I felt a lightness and a freedom I hadn't felt in months. Despite others' disapproval and disdain for my decision, I was being obedient to God and authentic to myself.

I stopped pretending to care about what didn't matter to me. I also stopped putting all my energy into gaining acceptance from those who didn't understand me, and I no longer spent my time trying to prove I wasn't what they thought about me. While I still craved friendship, I learned a valuable lesson: friendship isn't friendship if you can't be yourself, and friendship isn't worth it if it costs you your freedom.

Amos 3:3 says, "Can two people walk together without agreeing on the direction?"

FRIENDSHIP ISN'T FRIENDSHIP IF YOU CAN'T BE YOURSELF, AND FRIENDSHIP ISN'T WORTH IT IF IT COSTS YOU YOUR FREEDOM.

The answer to this rhetorical question is no. You can't walk with people who are heading toward a different destination. At some point, you'll be met with crossroads. At these crossroads, you'll have the choice between trekking the narrow road alone or following the broad path accompanied by others.

If you choose company over character, you will have to sacrifice your destination. You will forfeit your allegiance to God for the approval of people, surrendering your authenticity for the sake of acceptance. Simply put, the wrong company will cause you to compromise your SELF if you're not careful.

People-pleasing sends the message that your value to others comes only from how your actions can appease them;

God-pleasing sends the message that your value to others comes only from how your actions glorify God—regardless of what people think.

As a born-again Christian, you no longer share the same likeness as those living in darkness. You now carry the likeness and light of Christ through the indwelling of the Holy Spirit.

So while you may not detect the differences between yourself and someone else, the demons inside them recognize the Holy Spirit inside you. When demons feel threatened by Christ in you, it will inevitably cause friction. With untrained spiritual eyes, you may take offense at this. This rejection will make you believe that you don't belong or that you're unlikable, when the truth is that you *do* belong … You belong to Christ.

Jesus said it Himself in John 15:18–19, "If the world hates you, remember that it hated me first. The world would love you as one of its own if you belonged to it, but you are no longer part of the world. I chose you to come out of the world, so it hates you."

The message is clear—as Christians, we don't belong to this world. We belong to Christ. That's why, no matter how hard I tried to dim my light or mask my authenticity, I never seemed to blend in with the crowd. For some time, I didn't understand why, but experience was the best teacher. After many failed relationships with people who weren't walking the same path as me, God showed me this truth:

The reason you feel different is because you *are* different. Stop trying to deny your difference and learn to *embrace* it.

Becoming a Secure Connection

While I still yearned for friendships with women who met the same standard of Christlikeness, love, and respect that I kept within my relationship with Michael, I learned to first become it.

Each disappointing relationship made me better. I began to see that God was using the connections I labeled as "bad" for my good. He held each person up to me like a mirror, exposing the parts of me I had left to surrender to Him. The pain was like a fire burning away the impurities of self so I could look more like Him.

The people around me taught me how to love more deeply.

I began holding **myself** to an even higher standard. Higher levels of kindness. A stronger commitment to gentleness. A greater capacity for listening. A wider range for patience. Greater expressions of service.

It was no longer just about feeling like I'm the "bigger person" because I'm always the first to apologize or like I'm always being forgiving when others are holding a grudge. Because even that mentality kept score. Even that mentality was steeped in ego. Instead, it was about embracing the process of becoming everything God called me to be.

This is similar to the way God designed our immune systems to develop.

In attempts to help our kids avoid the pain of sickness, we could quarantine our children away from other kids, spray them down with sanitizer every five minutes, and never honor the "five-second rule" when their snacks hit the ground.

Sure, they'd rarely get sick, but they'd also become vulnerable and weak. Getting a cold and recovering from it would have benefitted them *far more* given that our immune systems were designed to develop as they learn to fight sickness. A kid with a strong immune system is one who experiences *more* of the world, not one who avoids it.

In the same way, hurtful experiences with people are an inevitable part of life. We can avoid them altogether to dodge disappointment, but then we'd never develop the character God has called us to have. Or instead, we can let them run their course and help us to become stronger, wiser, more loving, and more confident as a result.

If we let God do His work within us, experiences like these can shape us into confident women who offer secure connections to others. And because we're upholding this standard, we're able to ask for the same standard in return.

WE SHOULD ALL AIM TO SET A HIGH STANDARD FOR OURSELVES AND FOR OUR CONNECTIONS, BUT WE SHOULD ALSO EMBRACE THE JOURNEY OF GROWING ALONG THE WAY.

Embracing this journey of sanctification, I formed far more connections that shaped the trajectory of my life for the better. I began developing relationships with authentic people who truly love me as I am. These relationships are marked by safety, understanding, love, truth, and growth. They speak identity over me and push me toward my destiny.

I learned to keep a soft front while my back became stronger than ever. And the better I learned to love others, the more I attracted those who love well too. This could never have happened if I'd lived my life with a "no new friends" mentality in fear of getting hurt.

Relationships are sanctifying. They not only make us confident, but they also make us *holy*. We should all aim to set a high standard for ourselves and for our connections, but we should also embrace the journey of growing along the way. **This** is the inner work that we do to become who we're called to be.

REFLECT + PRAY

Reflect

- Are you involved in environments, groups, or relationships that may be headed in a different direction than you?
- How is God using the relationships in your life to shape your character?

Pray

- Thank God for the opportunity to connect with others. Specifically thank Him for the healthy relationships in your life.
- Ask God to give you wisdom and discernment about any relationships that could lead you in the wrong direction.

Spotting Insecure Connections

Spotting insecure connections isn't about labeling others as "bad" or "good."

It's not about pointing the finger, finding fault, or considering ourselves as "better than."

It's definitely not for the sake of showing others this book to say "aha!" and shame them.

The value in identifying the weak points within our personal connections is in improving the quality of them. The more confident, life-giving, loving, and Christlike we are, the more positively we can impact the lives of others.

Identifying insecure connections is our opportunity for introspection, surrender, and growth. God has given us the power to influence those around us for good. As we elevate our standards, we will also elevate those around us.

THREE MAJOR SIGNS OF INSECURE CONNECTIONS

1. The connection pulls you away from Christ.

- You're connected with unbelievers or compromised believers who negatively influence you or pressure you to abandon your devotion to Christ.
- You're connected with religious believers who pressure you to ascribe to their standards rather than giving you the freedom to follow the voice of God.
- The connection makes you question your faith in Christ or question your salvation.

- You sense the presence of darkness or evil around them.
- You feel obligated to please them above pleasing God.
- It influences you to "take steps backward" and digress.
- It reinforces the negative qualities you have and wish to change.
- Your stagnancy secures the connection, or your growth threatens the connection.

2. The connection isn't compatible with your values.
- The connection was aligned in your past but isn't aligned with your future.
- You don't align on values, convictions, or interests.
- The relationship doesn't seem to serve a lasting purpose.
- You don't agree on many life choices, which causes friction.
- The connection seems forced, one-sided, or incompatible.
- You are not challenged or sharpened by the connection.

3. The connection is unsafe.
- It is marked by manipulation or abuse.
- It is critical, judgmental, bitter, or unforgiving.
- It is aggressive or passive-aggressive.
- It is steeped in jealousy and competition.
- Gossip and slander have tainted the connection.
- It is dishonest, unpredictable, or volatile (with a lack of healthy conflict resolution).
- It plays mind games, or you feel like a pawn.
- It plays the blame game or keeps score.

- It feels one-sided, like there's no reciprocity.
- Your boundaries aren't respected.
- It has involved sabotage or betrayal.
- It makes you feel worse about yourself.
- You feel the constant need to prove or defend yourself.
- You no longer feel seen for who you are.

Chances are, if the connection feels unsafe, it is unsafe.

Seeking God's Perspective

Insecure connections have the ability to impact your confidence. However, spotting an insecure connection is not an immediate indication that the connection should be severed. Ending a relationship is serious business and shouldn't be taken lightly.

We live in the age of cancel, call-out, and cutoff culture. It's damaging for us to be negatively labeled, ostracized, or ghosted, so why would we do the same to others? The last thing believers need to do is throw people away in the name of "confidence." A truly confident woman will handle her connections—secure or not—wisely, lovingly, and gracefully.

The problems that we perceive in others can sometimes reveal the opportunities for growth within ourselves. When this happens, we have a choice. We can blame the other person for failing our expectations, or we can turn to God to see the situation from His perspective. Then, regardless of who's to blame, the situation welcomes us to be developed, sanctified, and refined.

Seeking God's perspective on navigating weaknesses within our connections addresses the root cause of relational insecurity:

uncertainty. Without an aerial view, insecure connections cause us to question everything. Our spirit and flesh duke it out for our soul as we swing back and forth between frustration and forgiveness, contempt and compassion. Especially if we're venting to every other ear and gleaning insight from every other voice but God's. In these situations, we can be left with mixed messages and feeling more unsure about things than when we started.

Bitterness, resentment, and animosity are exactly what we want to avoid. But too often, the fatigue of uncertainty leads to dissatisfaction within the relationship. Then, that unaddressed dissatisfaction can seep into how we treat the other person.

As we get God's perspective, He gives us **certainty**. He blesses us with the mindset we need to see others through the lens of love, insight into what is causing the relationship to sink, and wisdom on how to navigate it moving forward. This certainty leads to **confidence**.

Shifting Expectations

The more I've sought God about the people in my life, the healthier my relationships have become and the more confident I feel. He shows me which insecure connections to set new parameters for and which ones to end in due season, and He can do the same for you too.

My childhood best friend, Brittany, used to party with me, cheering me on in my sin and thinking nothing of it. Then, as I reconnected with God, she saw me change. Since our values stopped aligning, I could no longer consider the nature of the relationship reciprocal.

But I knew it wasn't right for me nix the friendship.

I could no longer spend weekends at her place, throwing on tight, skimpy dresses and a heavy smoky eye to carouse with strangers over obscene music and underage drinks. Not happening. But I could hear her out on her latest boy trouble, offer her Spirit-filled wisdom, be a shoulder to lean on, laugh with her over our stupid humor, train for a half-marathon together, and sit together at church on Sunday mornings.

So that's what I did.

Now, my friend didn't change immediately. Positively influencing her wasn't my only motive for connecting with her. I **loved** her. But eventually ... *she changed.*

The years flew by, and I had a front-row seat to watch God pull her out of darkness and into His glorious light. Without me ever having to wag my finger at her lifestyle, she rekindled her relationship with God, surrendered her old sin habits, and became wildly sold-out to the abundant life.

I tell you what: seeing this change in her not only made me surer of God's ability to work in the hearts of my loved ones, but it also made a once insecure connection **secure**—not by my own power but by God's.

I've seen it over and over again. It's not our job to change others. It's not our responsibility to convict others. We don't have the power to control others. Our role is to offer others **truth** and **love** as we let God handle the rest.

Jesus modeled the appropriate way to relate to others who couldn't benefit Him. Jesus didn't avoid sinners. He ate with them. It was **because** Jesus understood His role to impact sinners that He was able to reach people that the religious considered too far gone.

Keep in mind ...

Jesus didn't flirt with the woman at the well.

Jesus didn't hustle and rob people with the tax collectors.

Jesus didn't stick His nose up at sinners with the Pharisees.

Although Jesus extended Himself to sinners, He didn't allow their choices to affect His confidence or cause Him to compromise. Jesus set healthy parameters around His connections because He was led by His values and convictions. He used His time with others not to impress them but to **impact** them.

Jesus didn't connect to **get**. He connected to *give*.

In the same way, we can have healthy parameters around varying kinds of relationships by knowing what role we play in their lives. If a connection pulls you away from Christ, isn't compatible with your values, or is unsafe, it's your chance to learn God's perspective about it. He'll let you know if the connection needs some fresh boundaries and expectations or if the connection should be severed.

If you ask Him, He will show you.

REFLECT + PRAY

Reflect

- Have you been a secure connection in this person's life? Have you loved and supported others in the way Christ loves you?
- Is this truly an insecure connection that's pulling you away from Christ, or are you simply hurt, bothered, or offended?
- Have your actions damaged the connection? If so, have you apologized, changed your behavior, and repented for it?

Pray

- Ask God what His perspective is on each insecure connection in your life.
- Ask God for wisdom on how to appropriately navigate your insecure connections in light of this perspective.
- Pray for the power to avoid temptation and for the ability to be a light.
- Ask the Lord for the conviction to continue to be Christlike, confident, and uncompromised—even if it means others won't understand your choices.
- Pray for an ability to be loving, gracious, and gentle as you reframe relationships in your life.

When *Not* to Sever Connections

Offenses are a normal part of life. People will hurt us, and we will hurt people. That's a given.

But let it be known that there is a difference between someone having dangerous character flaws and someone making honest mistakes. The only way to know the difference is to watch their behavior. People show you who they are by what they **do**, not just by what they say.

A harmful person may say "sorry" yet continue their pattern of harm toward you. But a person who takes responsibility for offending you, apologizes, and changes their future actions toward you does not deserve the chopping block. In fact, their ability to respond humbly and sincerely usually identifies them as a **secure connection**.

Premature detachments are usually made in the heat of the moment, which is a clear sign of immaturity. Proverbs 19:11 says, "Sensible people control their temper; they earn respect by over-looking wrongs."

As we become secure, grounded women in Christ, we won't be riled by every offense that comes our way. We don't need to feel defensive, combative, or ruffled when others make mistakes. We will nurture the relationships by creating room for them to grow. As our confidence in Christ matures, it will empower us to confront offenses with truth and respond to the offender with grace.

The Bible says in Colossians 3:13, "Make allowance for each other's faults, and forgive anyone who offends you. Remember, the Lord forgave you, so you must forgive others."

Our confidence isn't proven in how quickly we can cut someone off or how little we need others. Christ's gift of new life by the Spirit is far richer than that. We prove our own integrity when we can take a good look in the mirror and give an honest assessment of ourselves, cultivating a genuine humility toward others.

True assurance in Christ says, "Because He graces me, I will grace you."

When to Sever Insecure Connections

Sometimes it's in the best interest of our mental health, safety, and healing to sever insecure connections entirely.

Women with a high level of self-worth won't negotiate with behaviors they should never tolerate. Because they know the value they offer to those around them, their threshold for toxic, harmful relationships is low.

Unfortunately, I've seen many Christian women assume it's "unloving" or "unforgiving" to do otherwise. For example, I've seen firsthand accounts of Christians remaining in spiritually abusive churches, believing their choice is a sign of their devotion to God. In cases like these, remaining in damaging relationships and environments is not as much an indication of self-worth as **wrong theology**.

Those with these theological misconceptions often quote the verses about forgiveness, not judging others, or even bearing one another's burdens while overlooking the ample number of passages that equip us with the wisdom we need to discern which relationships are worth keeping and which ones to avoid.

This message is well-meaning but *incomplete*.

Therefore, let me offer a biblical basis for ending relationships.

We've all heard the phrase "So-and-so is a person of character." We often use it as if a person's character couldn't change. The Bible tells us in 1 Corinthians 15:33, "Bad company corrupts good character." Therefore, even if a person has upright character, it doesn't mean their character will remain static. The biggest corruptor of character is the wrong connections.

This idea is solidified in other passages of Scripture.

Walk with the wise and become wise; associate with fools and get in trouble. (Prov. 13:20)

Don't befriend angry people or associate with hot-tempered people, or you will learn to be like them and endanger your soul. (Prov. 22:24–25)

We can see in these Scriptures that we can't afford to be naive. When we associate with the wrong people, it breaches our integrity and impacts our reputation. Every ounce of confidence we work toward can come crumbling to pieces if we fail to disconnect. Trust me, **I've lived it**.

Here's one more piece of biblical wisdom. Proverbs 18:24 says,

There are "friends" who destroy each other, but a real friend sticks closer than a brother.

Did you notice the word *friends* is in quotation marks when it's deemed as destructive? Then look at the contrast. When someone sticks closer than a brother, they are then regarded as a *real friend*.

We can see the sarcasm here. **Plainly** ... *Friends don't destroy friends.*

According to this proverb, we shouldn't consider those who are intentionally hurtful toward us "friends." We also shouldn't try to "stick close" to destructive people because, well, they're not *real* friends.

While God calls us to forgive without limit, He doesn't call us to connect without limit. As Christians, we aren't obligated to subject ourselves to blatantly unhealthy or abusive people. We are able to be loving and kind toward someone without giving them the access to compromise our character or crush our confidence.

In fact, sometimes the most loving, kind thing we can do for others is to **let them go**. As we release them, they are given the space to explore life without this unhealthy cycle they were once involved in.

So ... when should we sever insecure connections? The standard is simple.

If you've already established new parameters around a relationship—you've talked out offenses, you've forgiven any wrongs, you've set new boundaries, you've respectfully stated your expectations—yet the connection continues to negatively impact you, then it's time to remove yourself from that relationship. Severance is *especially* urgent in cases of abuse, damaging conflict resolution, consistent breaches of boundaries, sabotage, and betrayal.

How to Sever Insecure Connections

The decision to sever insecure connections doesn't mean we have to make the other person an enemy. Romans 12:18 tells us, "Do all that you can to live in peace with everyone." While we can't control how others respond to us ending a relationship, we can do our part to manage this transition in a way that is peaceful and civilized.

When it comes to ending relationships, I've made my fair share of mistakes. Yes, there have been clear instances when a connection of mine needed to be cut. But there have also been times when I went about it entirely wrong. I want to spare you from making those same mistakes by giving you some pointers.

Some relationships will sever on their own with time and distance. Others will require a clear cut. Prayer and wise counsel will show you the way.

First, pray to God and ask Him for wisdom on how to approach this specific connection. Write down any insights He reveals to you. Then share your concerns with your most trusted friend, leader, counselor, mentor, or your spouse. Also share what God revealed to you.

Finally, come to a consensus. Ensure that you, your trusted person, and God all agree on the next steps you will take with the connection in question.

If you, your trusted person, and God all agree that the right choice is to sever a connection, here are a few tips on following through that have helped me along my journey:

> - **Forgive** before you sever. Do not gossip about or slander the person you're disconnecting from. Make sure your heart is clear and your intentions are pure.
> - Set up a call with just the two of you. If the person has a history of volatility or aggression, include a mediator. **Do not sever a connection over text.** *In cases of abuse, seek professional counsel on ending a relationship.*
> - Don't list off every offense. Since you're not reconciling, it's not necessary to make the conversation about their wrongs. Instead, make it about the direction that God is taking you.
> - **Make the cut short, clear, and concise:** "Here are some things I've appreciated about our relationship … After praying and considering our relationship, I've learned that God is leading me in a new direction. I want to follow where He is taking me by closing this relationship."

‣ When they ask follow-up questions, continue to affirm them and remind them that this is less about their wrongs and more about where God is leading you.

‣ Finally, set the terms for the relationship moving forward: "I won't be reaching out or following you online, which is simply what's best for me moving forward. I understand this may hurt a little, but know that I'm praying the best for you, speaking well of you to others, and want you to have room for the right relationships too."

‣ *Stick* to it. Don't go back to anything you had to pray your way out of. After you've severed a connection, don't reach back out. Don't stalk them online. Be certain about your decision.

TAKE A STAND | CONNECT WITH OTHERS

Secure connections push you toward Christ, cultivate your calling, create a safe environment, and push you to grow. You'll know a connection is secure when it calls you to a higher level, pulls out the best in you, and secures your confidence. These connections are a gift from God that must be handled with care.

Once you've confirmed that your connections are safe, then it's time to categorize your connections, cultivate them, and create new ones. This will help you to feel even more secure by allowing you to manage expectations.

Categorize Your Connections

Make a list of all your connections, and place them in one of the following categories. Your connections will fall into Inner Circle, Outer Circle, or Impact Circle.

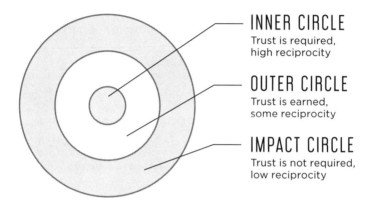

INNER CIRCLE
Trust is required,
high reciprocity

OUTER CIRCLE
Trust is earned,
some reciprocity

IMPACT CIRCLE
Trust is not required,
low reciprocity

After you've categorized your connections, make a written commitment to each circle that you will keep. This commitment will entail your expectations: what you will give to them and what you will get from them.

Inner Circle

Your **inner circle** consists of those who are closest to you, including your spouse or boyfriend. With these friendships, depth is more important than breadth. Your inner circle should rarely consist of more than a few **trustworthy** people you can go deep with. These relationships are about trust, vulnerability, and confidentiality.

Even Jesus understood this concept, having a circle of twelve disciples, with only three of those disciples—Peter, James, and John—belonging to His inner circle.

Example of a written commitment:

"I commit to give my inner circle my honesty, vulnerability, support, commitment, love, joy, respect, loyalty, and intentionality. I expect to get the same in return."

Outer Circle

Your **outer circle** consists of peers whose company you enjoy. These often become people that you invite to birthday parties, game nights, outings, and gatherings.

Your outer circle will also consist of acquaintances you're cordial with. You may see them around your neighborhood, at your church, at your gym, or elsewhere. You may not go much deeper than following each other on social media and brief conversations in passing.

Lastly, your outer circle will consist of strategic connections like mentors, coaches, or professional connections you've formed in your industry.

Example of a written commitment:

"I commit to give my outer circle my kindness, love, hospitality, and warmth. I expect respect in return."

Impact Circle

Your **impact circle** is the community that God placed you on this earth to positively influence. They're often within your vocational path or ministry reach, or those who share similar stories, desires, and passions. These can be members of your Bible study group, your followers on social media, those you disciple and mentor, and even your children. Lastly, you can serve your impact circle as clients and customers too.

God will use you to pull out the best in them by challenging their status quo, pushing them out of their comfort zones, and leading them by example. Your responsibility is to serve them even when they can't serve you. Your purpose is tied to people; therefore, if you don't have an impact community, then you're not fulfilling your purpose. You're called to create change within the lives of others.

Example of a written commitment:

"I commit to give my impact circle my wisdom, knowledge, positive example, and service. I expect respect in return."

Cultivate Your Connections

Jesus came to serve, not to be served. In the same way, we should cultivate our connections by serving them, not feeling entitled to them serving us. We serve others when we give.

Here are some practical ways to shift from the entitled mentality of "What can I get?" to "What can I give?"

TAKER'S MENTALITY	GIVER'S MENTALITY
Who is checking in on me?	I need to check on my friend.
Why am I not invited?	Let me invite her out with me.
No one is listening to me.	Let me hear you out.
They owe me.	Don't worry about it!
Who will celebrate me?	Let's send a gift to celebrate her.
My needs aren't being met.	I'm going to come by to help.
Who will support my vision?	I'm coming to support your event!
Everyone has their clique.	Hey! Come sit with us!

When you've been operating your relationships with a taker's mentality, you remain vulnerable to unmet expectations. This often leads to disappointment.

However, when you practice humility and generosity, treating others the way you'd want to be treated, not only will you experience higher levels of relational satisfaction, but you'll also radiate with confidence and attract the kind of connections you're craving.

Create New Connections

Whether you're hoping to get married to your purpose partner, build a lifelong inner-circle friendship, find an industry mentor, or simply meet new people in your area, intentionality is key. How you pick your people will reflect what you believe you deserve and will determine your destiny.

1. Pinpoint | Specify which new connections you're looking for.

Example: "I'm looking for an inner-circle friend to walk through life with."

2. Prioritize | List the top five values in your prospective connections.

Example: trustworthiness, honesty, laughter, growth mentality, reciprocity

3. Pray | Ask God to send the right connections your way.

Example: "Father, thank You for the gift of connection. I pray that You send me an inner-circle relationship, someone who is trustworthy, honest, and full of laugher, who has a growth mindset and shows reciprocity. Help me also to embody these values and be the type of person who can sustain this relationship. In Jesus' name, amen."

4. Position | Make yourself available to connect.

There is someone out there who has the same values and prayers for connection. Therefore, the standard you desire is the same standard you must demonstrate.

Get involved in environments that would attract the quality of connection you want. Church is often a great place to start. If you're looking to connect with other Christian women, you're invited to join our Confident Woman Community at www.confidentwomanco.com to find like-minded women in your area.

Competency

COMPONENT OF CONFIDENCE #3

The Importance of Competence

Competency is the third component of confidence. It's no secret that the more competent we are, the more confident we are.

If a person has studied in school to become competent at engineering, then they're more likely to be confident pursuing a career in engineering. However, if they've never studied engineering before and they pursue a career in engineering, they have no competency to base their confidence on.

The point is indisputable: confidence requires competency.

Now, this book isn't about becoming a confident engineer, a confident musician, or a confident mother. While this book offers frameworks that will help you to do so, those skills are not the focus. This book is about becoming a confident woman in Christ.

Spiritual confidence is the only form of confidence that affects all other forms of confidence. So in this chapter, we'll tackle how to become so spiritually sharp that no matter what environment we walk into, we can stand in confidence.

This section of the book will equip you to become spiritually confident by targeting two skills:

> ▸ **Expand Your Capacity** | Know Healing and Deliverance
> ▸ **Sharpen Your Ability** | Reclaim Your Confidence

Chapter 5

EXPAND YOUR CAPACITY

Make Room for More

Confidence requires capacity.

The less **capacity** we hold for belief, the less we experience in life. The more we believe, the more we experience in life.

If we want more out of life, then we must make room for more. If we receive more but don't have room for more, then the overflow becomes a burden, not a blessing.

Think about it this way …

First, God created the heavens and the earth.

Then He separated the sky from the water.

Then He put birds in the air and fish in the sea.

God didn't create stars without first stretching a sky to hold them.

He didn't design fish without first expanding a sea to hold them.

The capacity was created **first** with the belief and hope that good things would come. Then that space was filled.

In the same way, greater confidence calls for greater capacity. When we want God to expand us, our prayer should be, "Lord, create in me capacity."

Without capacity, we may **receive**, but we will not have space to **retain** all the good things God brings our way. This is why we see people who get rich quickly but squander it just as quickly—they didn't have the internal capacity to receive the very thing they'd hoped for. They received wealth, but they didn't remain wealthy.

WHEN WE WANT GOD TO EXPAND US, OUR PRAYER SHOULD BE, "LORD, CREATE IN ME CAPACITY."

In our efforts to become more confident, it's vital that we learn what could potentially drain our confidence once we get it. Expanding our capacity for more will not only help us **receive** confidence but it'll also help us **retain** confidence. And the sign of a good and faithful servant is not just one who receives much; the sign of a good servant is one who gets a **return** on what they receive.

To create more capacity for confidence, we need to first **remove** what is draining our confidence.

Satan uses two main confidence drainers in our lives:

▸ Unhealed wounds
▸ The fear of people

In this chapter, we will learn how to spot the Enemy's strategy to use these two things to make us sink in insecurity. Then we will learn how to expand our capacity to stand confidently in our God-given identity.

Confidence Drainer #1 | Unhealed Wounds

Time alone does not heal all wounds. Unaddressed hurts reduce our capacity and therefore hinder our confidence. When we experience life through the lens of **past** defeat, disappointment, loss, and pain, it stifles our ability to see the **new** thing God is doing in us and through us.

Signs that unhealed wounds are killing your capacity include:

- You feel emotionally unavailable to grow beyond your current state.
- You feel disappointed or hurt in relation to yourself, God, or others.
- You accept defeat and choose not to fight for yourself in everyday scenarios.
- You continue to dabble in secret sin because you still identify with your shame.
- You accept and maintain damaging relationships and repeat damaging cycles.
- You withhold forgiveness from others and yourself.
- You wallow in shame and condemnation.
- You rehearse the memory of your pain, don't feel closure, or haven't moved on from past hurts.

Do any of these signs resonate with you? If so, then you likely have unhealed wounds that need to be addressed.

Together, let's learn the Enemy's strategy to limit our capacity through unhealed wounds. Then we'll form a new strategy to heal the wounds with Christ so we can make room for what God has for us next.

Recognize the Enemy's Strategy for Limiting Capacity through Unhealed Wounds

1. **Open Door:** First, a traumatic event happens in our lives. This event becomes an open door, a point of entry for false messengers to enter.
2. **Entry:** These messengers tell us lies about ourselves, lies about God, lies about others, and lies about our future.
3. **Damage:** If these messengers are not challenged with a true narrative, then we accept their narrative as our own faulty framework of belief. This creates a pattern of negative behaviors and insatiable insecurity, resulting in self-sabotage, rejected opportunities for growth, and more.

These continued cycles reduce our capacity. And with limited capacity, we stop believing, hoping, and trusting in a brighter future.

God offers all of us abundant life, but that requires healing. Psalm 34:18 tells us, "The LORD is close to the brokenhearted; he rescues those whose spirits are crushed." He cares about the condition of your heart and watches over the state of your soul. He longs for your joy and prays for your peace. God wants you to heal so you can make room for the abundant blessings He offers you.

Recognize God's Strategy for Healing

1. **Open Door:** We approach Jesus with the pain of the traumatic event in our lives, either as the event is happening or after. This open door becomes an entry point for His messenger—His Spirit—to enter.

2. **Entry:** His Spirit shines light and truth, combatting the false narrative and helping us to see life through the lens of victory.

3. **Restoration:** The painful event that could have destroyed us becomes the event that refines us. We are sanctified, proven, and restored because of it. As a result, greater measures of wisdom and truth flow from us. We are able to love our enemies, pray for those who persecute us, and offer healing through Christ to others. What the Enemy sent as a stumbling block becomes our stepping-stone. We are confident that the hardships we faced are preparing us to steward and multiply what God has in store for us next.

You can seek healing with the support of therapy, conversation with trusted loved ones, medical treatment, and more. God has given us these resources, but He alone is the source. Don't seek those things without Him.

God sent Jesus to die for our freedom. He doesn't want us bound to our past, our inner critic, our fear, or our wounds. If He were content with us living in depression, lust, and bitterness, then He would have never sent Jesus to rescue us. The Scripture is clear that we have been set free from sin; however, we must shed the mindset of slavery and sin, even if that shedding comes little by little, season by season.

Understand that healing is not passive—it's active. This is why you'll see fifty-year-old people who are still bitter, immature, and angry—they hold on to beliefs and hurts from when they were younger. As a result, unhealed wounds may have been limiting their capacity for decades, preventing them from claiming the truth, freedom, and abundance God has offered them.

Addressing the Enemy's negative messages and revisiting the painful experiences that opened the door to them requires intentionality and bravery. You have the power to confront these messages, close the open doors, and find restoration. The choice is yours.[1]

Now let's include Christ in your healing journey so that you will experience the level of freedom and confidence you've been praying for.

TAKE A STAND | EMOTIONAL HEALING

Let's examine the five-part healing framework that I've walked many women through to help them grow in emotional freedom. It is the same framework I follow myself.

1. Acknowledge the Messengers

First, pray to invite God into this healing process with you. Ask His Spirit to guide this experience, shine His light, and bring you true freedom.

Next, think of the most painful messages you've learned in life. These are false messages about you, God, or others. There will likely be more than one, so we will tackle them one at a time. Choose **one** for this exercise.

At the top of a fresh journal page, write down one negative message and the primary emotions this message triggered.

Examples of false messages and the emotions tied to each:

Self: "I am the problem in all my relationships, and I will always be the reason they fail." This made me feel **disapproval** and **shame** about who I am.

Others: "Men are cruel and unsafe. I need to think ten steps ahead to protect myself." This made me feel **vulnerable** and **distrusting**.

God: "God is holding out on me, and others will always have it better than me. I will always be at a disadvantage, and this is God's plan." This made me feel **inferior** and **jealous**.

To help pinpoint your specific emotion, refer to the Emotions Wheel by Dr. Albert Wong (www.dralbertwong.com /feelings-wheel).[2] This wheel is an incredibly strong resource that can help you pinpoint your emotions so that you can delve deep and then move forward. As you examine the wheel, one or two prevalent emotions will stand out to you with each message.

As you go through this discovery process, don't reason with your feelings by explaining them away or intellectualizing them ... Simply feel them. Tell God how you feel too.

2. Find the Open Door

Think back to the very first time you ever felt these specific emotions. This will correlate with a life event. The event could be recent or as far back as your childhood. All that matters is that you indicate the very first time you felt them.

Remember every detail you may have forgotten. Before you write anything down, close your eyes to replay and relive that moment. If this still hurts, it's a sign that you're addressing the root of the problem.

Write down the painful accounts of this emotion you recall, from earliest to most recent.

Examples of times you felt *anxious* and *overwhelmed*:

First occurrence: "When I was in kindergarten and was behind in my reading skills, my dad kept snapping at me and pressuring me to improve."

Next occurrence: "When I was in third grade and I got my first B on a test, my mom punished me by giving me the silent treatment. We didn't speak for days."

Another occurrence: "When I was in high school, I didn't get the test scores that would qualify me for the college of my dreams. When I took the tests again, my scores still didn't improve, and my parents blamed me for not trying hard enough."

Once you have a collection of events, you can see where your pain was introduced and reinforced. Make note of the pattern. This exposes the Enemy's strategy to derail you.

Example of the Enemy's pattern across time:
"The Enemy used the times I underperformed academically to make me doubt my worth and value to my parents. This limited my capability to succeed by causing me to lack confidence."

Most people I've led through this exercise have remembered three to six events associated with each emotion. You'll usually find a trend or theme in the messages you were sent when these emotions surfaced.

3. Let God In

Now that the door is wide open again, this is your opportunity to let the Holy Spirit in.

Ask God to reveal to you the truth about these situations; then give Him room to **answer**. Sit in silence, and take note of everything that you see, hear, notice, imagine, remember, sense, and feel. He often will bring Scripture to mind. This is God communicating with you. He wants to reveal to you more about His love for you and His plan for you.

Example of God's revelations:

"God reminded me that my parents have a works-based view of worth and value, which they projected onto me. But God's love is different. It's not based on how well I perform or achieve. His perfect love casts out all fear … even fear of being a failure."

Write down whatever He reveals to you, and don't question it. Thank Him for His truth.

4. Forgive

Unforgiveness also hinders us deeply. In the same way that Jesus healed and forgave us to purchase our freedom, ongoing healing and forgiveness work together to free us. Forgiveness is an action. It's resolving not to hold a grudge, harbor resentment, cling to hatred, or withhold love.

Who caused these feelings in you? Write down their name(s).

Then verbally release each person one at a time and pray for them:

I forgive _____ for _____ . I will no longer keep a record of their wrongs against me, hold a grudge, or harbor bitterness, hatred, or resentment. I free them from all mental, emotional, spiritual, financial, physical, and any other debt they owe me. They owe me nothing. I forgive them.

Father, I release _____ to You and entrust them to Your hands. I commit to not seek revenge because I trust You with my future. I pray that You would bless _____. *(Pray a specific prayer of blessing.)*

5. Receive

If you could replace the negative emotion with any other positive emotion, what would it be? Perhaps you'd rather replace feelings of rejection with feelings of **acceptance**.

Write down the emotion that would truly satisfy the void in your heart.

Then pray this prayer:

"Jesus, Your Scripture says that You were whipped so we could be healed. So please heal me. Replace my feelings of _____ with feelings of_____."

Examples of prayer for new emotions:
"Jesus, Your Scripture says that by Your stripes I am healed. So please heal me. Replace my feelings of shame with feelings of **worthiness**."

"Jesus, Your Scripture says that by Your stripes I am healed. So please heal me. Replace my feelings of not being enough with feelings of **confidence**."

After following this framework, assess how you feel. Are the negative feelings gone? Do you feel lighter?

Usually, undergoing this process of healing leaves a person feeling lighter. Many describe themselves as feeling at ease, at peace, or resolved afterward. When someone doesn't feel the shift, then it's clear: there are underlying emotions that have yet to be acknowledged and processed. Because pain and trauma bring about a complex cocktail of sentiments, this is completely normal. Whenever the most prevalent feelings associated with an event are addressed, it opens up opportunity for the varying residual emotions to be dealt with.

It may be a feeling of unworthiness, abandonment, or anything else. Identify that emotion immediately, and then go through the process of emotional healing again. Continue to do this until you feel your past wounds healing and your capacity for love, acceptance, and confidence expanding. Be sure to let God lead you through each of these steps with an open heart.

Confidence Drainer #2 | The Fear of People

If we spend just five minutes in conversation with friends, streaming social media, or watching the news, we're bombarded with other people's ideas, opinions, and pressures. When we crave their acceptance, approval, and validation more than God's, we begin to follow them instead of Him.

Who are we without all that noise from the world?

What social issues would we champion if our political party didn't exist?

What clothes would we wear if social media didn't influence us?

What would we believe without feedback from all these outside voices?

The thing is, if we feel confident only when we're satisfying societal standards, then we're not truly confident; we're compromised.

Proverbs 29:25 says, "Fearing people is a dangerous trap, but trusting the LORD means safety."

Why does this verse mention **fear**? Because we will follow those whose disapproval we fear most. For this reason, the Bible teaches us to "fear the Lord"—because then we will follow His perfect plan for our lives.

Signs that the fear of man is limiting your capacity:

▸ You have trouble identifying your own convictions, thoughts, and opinions.

▸ You perform, people-please, or lack boundaries.

▸ You're held to religious regulations and legalism to appease people in your church.

▸ You shape-shift depending on who you think others want you to be.

▸ You lack confidence to make decisions without someone else's approval.

▸ You fear disapproval from people more than you fear disapproval from God.

▸ You feel like you're crumbling under the weight of others' expectations of you.

None of these experiences are God's will for your life. If you are sinking in insecurity because of the fear of man, then it will drain you of the capacity to confidently pursue God's plan for your life.

The Enemy's Strategy to Harm Us

Rather than following the voice of the Good Shepherd, we can end up following the voice of a stranger. And while some strangers may have our best interests in mind, others may be "hired hands" or, worse, "wolves in sheep's clothing."

Jesus says in John 10:

> I am the good shepherd. The good shepherd sacrifices his life for the sheep. A hired hand will run when he sees a wolf coming. He will abandon the sheep because they don't belong to him and he isn't their shepherd. And so the wolf attacks them and scatters the flock. The hired hand runs away because he's working only for the money and doesn't really care about the sheep. (vv. 11–13)

Let's break this down.

First Jesus tells us He is the Good Shepherd and we are His sheep. Only a good shepherd would be willing to die for the sake of his sheep. Jesus is that devoted to protecting us, so His voice will always steer us in the right direction.

When Jesus says, "a hired hand will run when he sees a wolf coming," that's something worth taking seriously because the wolf represents the Devil. Like the wolf that prowls among the sheep, the Devil is always out there, seeking to devour us.

Now let's explore this concept of a "hired hand." In Scripture, hired hands are representative of spiritual leaders who are "false teachers" and "false prophets."

Peter the apostle warned about these leaders in 2 Peter 2:1–3:

> There were also false prophets in Israel, just as there will be false teachers among you. They will cleverly teach **destructive** heresies and even deny the Master who bought them. In this way, they will bring sudden **destruction** on themselves. Many will follow their evil teaching and shameful immorality. And because of these teachers, the way of truth will be slandered. In their greed they will make up clever lies to get hold of your money. But God condemned them long ago, and their **destruction** will not be delayed.

Who else destroys?

The thief; the Enemy; *the Devil.*

So I'll say it straight. If someone is a false prophet, they're following the Devil. Don't follow their path; it was paved to destroy you.

A hired hand isn't just a spiritual leader; a hired hand is a spiritual principle. When you open the door to fear—namely, the fear of man—then anyone who influences you can become a hired hand and destroy you.

- an influencer, politician, celebrity, author, leader, teacher, or boss you admire
- a friend, coworker, classmate, or family member whose opinion you fear more than God's

‣ a political party, worldview, cultural norm, movement, denomination, or any other voice that influences your choices

But the good news is that despite the many dangers that surround us, Jesus is our Good Shepherd. He came to set us free!

When the Holy Spirit is working through us, we're no longer ruled or defined by everyone else's expectations—we're defined by God.

The spiritual realm exists, and as believers we can't ignore it. If we've already given our lives to Christ, we must make a conscious decision to continue to follow His Spirit—no other spirit ... His voice—no other voice.

THE SPIRITUAL REALM EXISTS, AND AS BELIEVERS WE CAN'T IGNORE IT.

Once a spirit other than the Holy Spirit has the access to influence us, then we're no longer in alignment. Instead of experiencing peace, freedom, and power, we're experiencing loss and ruin instead.

To combat this spiritual force called "the fear of man" that pressures us to follow hired hands, we must engage in spiritual warfare. **Spiritual warfare** is the act of spiritual fighting against demonic spirits that attempt to keep us from fulfilling God's calling. Spiritual warfare is essential for us to walk in **freedom** and operate in **power**.

God's Strategy to Free Us
1. Identify and Reject the Spirit

As children of God, our bodies are temples inhabited by the Holy Spirit. However, even though the Holy Spirit protects us from being *possessed* by demons, we can still be *oppressed* by them. But 2 Corinthians 3:17–18 tells us how to protect ourselves from such oppression:

> The Lord is the Spirit, and wherever the Spirit of the Lord is, there is **freedom**. So all of us who have had that veil removed can see and reflect the glory of the Lord. And the Lord—who is the **Spirit**—makes us more and more like him as we are changed into his glorious image.

This passage highlights that the Lord is a Spirit who brings us freedom.

But let's consider this closely. If this Holy Spirit makes us "more and more" like God … then what spirit is influencing us to look more and more like other people?

In the latter case, the spirit of fear—specifically the fear of people—is the spiritual force pressuring us to follow hired hands and robbing us of our inner freedom.

2. Close the Open Door

We grant demonic spirits access through open doors:

▸ Unhealed wounds or traumatic events in our lives

▸ Habitual sins like unforgiveness, bitterness, envy, jealousy, anger, hatred, strife, vanity, selfishness, lust, greed, or offense

▸ The sins of our ancestors (Ex. 20:4–6)

The good news is we have authority over any evil spirit through the power of Jesus.

3. Surrender to God's Spirit

All we need to do is surrender to the Holy Spirit.

The Holy Spirit is our secret weapon that helps us resist sin, do the work of God, and use our spiritual gifts. Jesus made this clear to His disciples in John 16:7–8, 13–15:

I tell you the truth. **It is to your advantage that I go away; for if I do not go away, the Helper will not come to you; but if I depart, I will send Him to you**. And when He has come, He will convict the world of sin, and of righteousness, and of judgment....

When He, the **Spirit of truth**, has come, He will **guide you into all truth;** for He will not speak on His own authority, but whatever He hears He will speak; and He will tell you things to come. He will glorify Me, for He will take of what is Mine and declare it to you. All things that the Father has are Mine. Therefore I said that He will take of Mine and **declare it to you**. (NKJV)

See? Jesus made it clear in His own words, saying it's a good thing that He ascended back to heaven because, afterward, He sent us our secret weapon. The Holy Spirit is our Helper who will guide us into all truth. With the Holy Spirit, we are never alone.

This means that if you surrender your struggles and temptations to the Spirit, He will help you overcome them.

If you surrender your battles to the Spirit, He will help you win them.

If you surrender your pain and heartache to the Spirit, He will help you heal them.

Surrendering to the voice of the Holy Spirit may be scary if you've formed a habit of relying on hired hands, so I'll share my story to give you hope.

HE DOES NOT INCITE IN ME THE PRESSURE TO PERFORM. INSTEAD, HE BUILDS IN ME THE CONFIDENCE TO STAND.

When I sought God for freedom from hired hands in my life, I expected Him to shake His finger at me and remark, "You should have known better." While that wasn't the character of the God I served, I'd fused people's disapproval of me with the Lord's. Layer by layer, God peeled back the mound of rigid expectations that had entrapped me, and He met me with kindness, affirmation, and truth.

While in prayer, I heard God speak these words over me:

Daughter, I love you so much and I cherish you. I love being gentle with you and pursuing you. It's supposed to be that way. Let Me in.

I am for you and not against you. I will fight for your peace and nurture you back to life. I am your ever-constant defender. You are safe with Me, daughter, and My will for you is to heal.

The Enemy is trying to make you fall, but I've called you to stand. Through Me, you're going to stand. Know that I see all things, and I haven't changed My mind about you. My love for you is unconditional, and My call is clear. I need you to accept that call and reject other options.

I have a wonderful plan for you. Just trust Me.

Time after time, the Lord has guided me truthfully and shepherded me tenderly. He knows that I need Him, so when I've met Him for prayer and worship, He has showered me with His healing presence. As I pray and read His Word, I am reminded that He does not incite in me the pressure to perform. Instead, He builds in me the confidence to stand.

God has shown me that He is the Good Shepherd who laid down His life for me.

And you know what? He's done the same for you.

His intentions for you are **good**. When you trust in Him, everyone will know that it was God who has opened your heart and brought blessings your way. His hand on your life and His imprint on your story will be undeniable to all. He's just waiting on your surrender. Trust, and let Him in.

TAKE A STAND | ENGAGE IN WARFARE

1. Confront

I've heard it said that prayer is not only communion with God—it is confrontation with the enemy. We must take authority over every demonic influence in our lives through prayer, Scripture, and declaring the name of Jesus.

To conquer the spirit of fear, pray this prayer:

Lord, I confront the spirit of fear in my life. It is written in Acts 5:29 that "we must obey God rather than any human authority." I declare that I will only obey You.

Through the power of the mighty name of Jesus, I denounce all forms of fear of man, including the fear of rejection, intimidation, loneliness, abandonment, mistreatment, and disapproval.

I stand confidently in Psalm 118:6, which says, "The LORD is on my side; I will not fear. What can man do to me?" (NKJV). Lord, You will never leave me or forsake me.

Break off all ties with any hired hands in my life, including false prophets, false teachers, influencers, celebrities, leaders, teachers, authorities, friends, coworkers, classmates, relatives, political parties, worldviews, movements, denominations, or any other voice that counters Your truth. The alliance is severed by the name of Jesus.

Your Word says in Proverbs 9:10 that "Fear of the Lord is the foundation of wisdom." Therefore, I will fear You only and follow in Your will and way.

2. Repent

"If we confess our sins, he is faithful and just and will forgive us our sins and purify us from all unrighteousness" (1 John 1:9 NIV).

God's Spirit empowers us to change. But first we must repent of our sins.

Repentance begins with a stirring of deep sorrow or regret. But with true repentance, this remorse leads not only to confession but also to lasting changes in our behavior.

If applicable, write down the sins you've committed that led to this emotional pain. Be honest about where you've gone wrong, and believe that God's power will help you to do right.

Then pray this to confess these sins to God and ask for His forgiveness:

Father, I take responsibility for giving access to the spirit of fear. I repent for idolizing other people over You. I was wrong. I thank You for forgiving me through the blood of Jesus. Let Your Spirit change me so that I can accomplish Your will.

3. Receive

God's Spirit is most powerful in your SURRENDER.

The moment you believe in Christ, you receive His Holy Spirit. When you receive the Holy Spirit, you no longer strive in your own strength; you STAND in God's strength. You no longer operate in your own willpower; you operate in God's power. You are no longer limited by your weaknesses, because where you're weak, He is strong.

Now is your opportunity to ask the Holy Spirit to lead and guide you in life.

First, write down every area in your life that was not surrendered to the Holy Spirit, including areas that other people were leading you in and areas in which you were leading yourself.

Then pray this prayer:

Father, thank You for being the Good Shepherd who will never lead me astray. Thank You for giving me Your Holy Spirit to lead and guide me in my everyday decisions.

Give me eyes to see the path You've paved for me and ears to hear Your voice leading me. I surrender these areas to You: (list all areas).

I commit to no longer follow the voice of any person and will instead follow the voice of the Holy Spirit. Thank You for assuring me that I'm not alone in this and that You're with me every step of the way. In Jesus' name, amen.

Finally, receive His voice. Sit in silent expectation for God to communicate with you. Whatever He is speaking over you, write it down and believe it.

Remember that the voice of God will never contradict the Word of God. So you can have confidence that God is communicating with you when His voice aligns with Scripture.

Repairing any unhealed wounds and overcoming our fear of man is something we must all do to grow in confidence. But when we make this shift, we will yield a return that will continue for all eternity.

Chapter 6

SHARPEN YOUR ABILITY

The Chemistry of Confidence

Whether within the workforce, academic environments, family systems, or elsewhere, it's no secret that women have been conditioned by our culture to think less of ourselves. In turn, this causes us to overwork to prove our worth to the world.

By the time we finally recognize the need to change our mindset, we've already created a lifestyle of insecurity, self-sabotage, performance, and perfectionism. This can become so ingrained in our brains that our cells physically conform to our beliefs, emotions, and thoughts—and our actions obey them! When we decide to see ourselves accurately through Christ, we can replace our patterns of insecurity with a lifestyle of confidence.

This will require us to become even more capable of believing that in Christ we're worthy of love and belonging and then gladly accepting the good He sends our way. When we do this by way of our faith, focus, feelings, and follow-through, our new baseline will be marked by love, acceptance, hope, joy, and peace.

When I began my confidence journey, I had to challenge my previously held perceptions of love and life and actively replace them with Christ-centered beliefs. Over time, what once was a pattern of loss and regret became a pattern of growth and satisfaction.

Where I once rejected goodness because of my feelings of shame and inadequacy, I now received it because of my belief that I was worthy and deserving of it. As I accepted good things like healthy relationships, greater levels of purpose, and better opportunities, the feedback confirmed my new framework.

In this chapter, we will discuss how to uproot our insecurities and replace them with confidence that will last.

We will do this by following the **Reclaim Your Confidence Framework** to build a new infrastructure for rock-solid confidence.

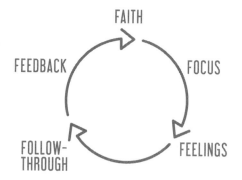

1. **Faith** | Reprogram Your Beliefs
2. **Focus** | Renew Your Thoughts and Words

3. **Feelings** | Review Your Emotions
4. **Follow-through** | Revise Your Actions
5. **Feedback** | Receive Your Reward

After we discuss the five factors of the framework, you'll have directives to immediately take a stand. Make it your highest priority not to simply read this section but to apply it with follow-through. This is the only way you'll truly change your life for good.

1. Faith | Reprogram Your Beliefs

Think of faith as the internal programming of a computer keyboard. Say you drop a keyboard and all the keys fall off. Then when you reassemble the keyboard, you accidentally place the *O* where the *A* belongs. As a result, even when you type the correct pattern for *apple*, the keyboard will continue to produce the word *opple*.

In the same way, your faith functions as your internal programming. It is what you believe to be most true, even subconsciously. You live by laws based on your perception of the world. Even if you want to behave more confidently, if you haven't reprogrammed your faith, your efforts will not match your outcomes.

One thing that can impact our programming is the environment we were raised in. We may reject some of it, but we often keep more of what our parents taught us about the way life works than we may recognize. We are also programmed by our society and culture. Much of society runs by a similar mental rulebook—and many of the rules are not rooted in truth.

THROUGH THE RENEWING POWER OF SCRIPTURE, THE SPIRIT GIVES US SOUND MINDS, ENABLING US TO MAKE HEALTHIER DECISIONS IN ALIGNMENT WITH OUR DESTINY.

For this very reason, Romans 12:2 says, "Do not conform to the pattern of this world, but be transformed by the renewing of your mind. Then you will be able to test and approve what God's will is—his good, pleasing and perfect will" (NIV).

Lies are so pervasive in the world around us that we accept them to be the very faith through which we navigate life ... and then we wonder why we're so insecure!

One myth many people believe is that our beliefs can't be changed. But that's not even remotely true. We each hold the ability to update our internal software anytime we want. We can choose to replace our insecurities with confidence, but this process will require us to reprogram our beliefs about ourselves, God, and others.

We do this by challenging our existing programming and replacing it through the study, meditation, and declaration of **Scripture** and truth. Through the renewing power of Scripture, the Spirit gives us sound minds, enabling us to make healthier decisions in alignment with our destiny.

2. Focus | Renew Your Thoughts and Words

The validity of our faith is revealed by the quality of our focus. By the time we think the thoughts or speak the words, we've given them our **focus**. Without an overhaul, this focus is the energy we employ to reinforce the faulty frameworks that have been causing us to sink in insecurity. Then our lives become a reaction to our thoughts and words.

The Bible confirms this cause and reaction in Romans 8:5–6:

> Those who are dominated by the sinful nature think about sinful things, but those who are controlled by the Holy Spirit think about things that please the Spirit. So letting your sinful nature control your mind leads to death. But letting the Spirit control your mind leads to life and peace.

We see "death" in our lives as insecurity, self-sabotage, and overall darkness. When this happens, we can likely trace it back to the thoughts produced from our minds and the words produced from our mouths.

This is why we must be mindful of what we think about. This is called *metacognition*.

Our thoughts are thoughts. Nothing more. We often assume our thoughts to be true because we don't create enough space to step back and recognize them as mere "thoughts," much less challenge them. It's key to remember that we don't have to accept every thought as true. Nor do we have to react emotionally to our thoughts or behave in certain ways based on our thoughts. We can simply allow them to rise like emotions, look at them objectively, and discard any that don't serve God.

Scripture also confirms our ability to reject our thoughts in 2 Corinthians 10:4–5, which reads, "We use God's mighty weapons, not worldly weapons, to knock down the strongholds of human reasoning and to destroy false arguments. We destroy every proud obstacle that keeps people from knowing God. We capture their rebellious thoughts and teach them to obey Christ."

Crazy thoughts will come ... that's a given. We don't have to punish ourselves every time we think low about ourselves or feel pressured to find confidence according to the world's standards. But we do have the power to destroy that reasoning and train our thoughts to obey Christ through Scripture and the power of the Holy Spirit.

Additionally, the brain doesn't distinguish truth from lies ... It only responds to commands. So COMMAND your life by commanding your thoughts!

When your thoughts become words ... that's when they hold real power.

Romans 10:9–10 shows us how powerful our combined words and beliefs are. It says,

> If you **confess with your mouth** that Jesus is Lord and **believe in your heart** that God raised him from the dead, you will be saved. For with the heart one believes and is justified, and with the mouth one confesses and is saved. (ESV)

This Scripture confirms that our words hold the power of life and death. What we speak about ourselves, others, and God determines the course of our lives. If our thoughts and words determine our eternal destination, then they're the most powerful force we possess.

When we underestimate the power of our words, we may not recognize that our insecurities have stemmed from words we've confessed about ourselves. This could look like ...

A woman who constantly calls herself "ugly" and so, over time, she's stopped caring for her health or hygiene.

Or ...

A woman who confesses, "I am a failure," and then begins squandering every opportunity that comes her way and rejecting any chance of growth.

I used to make statements like, "There's something wrong with me."

Because of this, I would always highlight my own deficiencies instead of celebrating my strengths. Even though I wanted to become more confident, these words backfired on me because I began enhancing the power of my weaknesses and diminishing the power of my strengths. This pattern only stunted my competency and sent negative messages to me about my self-efficacy.

When I chose to lead a more confident life, I replaced self-destructive words with affirmations. (We will cover this in greater detail when we take a stand.)

For now, the key is that we must challenge our thoughts *before* they become words. The only words we want to speak are the ones we'd like to see manifest in our lives. If we don't want to see it happen, we will not say it.

REFLECT + PRAY

Reflect

- Where does your mind wander when it's at rest?
- What gets most of your focus and why?
- Do the words you speak match the life you want to live?

Pray

- Thank God for giving you the mind of Christ and the ability to accept His thoughts instead of your own.
- Ask Him to give you a greater awareness of the thoughts you think and to sharpen your response by submitting every rebellious thought to His truth.
- Ask God to show you how to guard your mouth and season your words with salt.
- Ask the Holy Spirit to speak through you, calling forth life for yourself and those around you.

3. Feelings | Review Your Emotions

We feel the way we feel because of the thoughts we think. In other words, what we focus on determines how we feel.

Many people, particularly women, tend to struggle to compartmentalize their internal feelings and their external reality, making them more likely to accept their emotions as truth.

Personally, I lean more toward being a feeler than a thinker. Because I feel my emotions so intensely, it can seem as if my feelings precede my thoughts.

In the past, I lacked the self-awareness to question the source of my feelings before reacting to them. After intentionally sharpening my emotional intelligence (EQ)[1] over time, I gained the awareness to process my emotions before empowering them.

While I still struggle at times to bear the intensity of my feelings, especially when they're related to what I feel about myself, I've learned to slow down to inspect them. I used to hate being so "emotional," and even labeled myself negatively because of it. But my counselor helped me reframe the way I viewed emotions.

She told me that emotions are not bad; they're simply indicators like check-engine lights. When we feel negative emotions, we're not supposed to resent them or ignore them. That doesn't resolve the underlying problem. Just as we inspect the engine when a check-engine light is on, we're supposed to inspect our emotions and address the root issue so that we remain healthy. We do this by finding the thoughts—whether explicit or subconscious—that are triggering them.

Whenever I am triggered with negative emotions, I've learned to ask myself, *Why do I feel this way?*

Once I identify the underlying thought that is causing me pain, I ask the Lord for His perspective and receive lasting relief and truth.

WHAT WE FOCUS ON
DETERMINES HOW WE FEEL.

For many years, I would only approach God to gain His insight about my pain after experiencing the thick of it. I'd spiral and sink under the weight of unbearable pain, vent to others about it, ruminate over it, and try to resolve it without God. After experiencing the worst of it … even reaching the point of self-harm and ideating death … *then* I would seek the Lord.

Rookie mistake.

My conflict resolution skills, emotional processing skills, and self-management skills started drastically improving when I stopped seeking God **after** I was sinking and started pursuing Him **while** I was sinking. That's when I learned that timing is everything!

Some things I perceived as big problems were actually small problems because my spiritual immaturity had limited my perspective.

Over time, I stopped asking myself, "Why do I feel this way?" and started asking, "God, what're You showing me?" This simple shift took me to an entirely different level of spiritual maturity.

By seeing my problems from God's perspective, I was finally able to see how small my problems truly were. Then I could move through the negative experiences and reclaim joy, peace, hope … and sleep just fine at night.

I learned that God doesn't dismiss our struggles and pain; He delights in meeting us in the middle of the mess. With Him, I'm able to receive fatherly comfort, *rhema* words of wisdom, and fresh perspective. I don't have to revel in lies for hours or days before standing in the truth. I can get immediate relief as I seek Him in the moment.

This is yet another reason Psalm 34:18 tells us that "The LORD is close to the brokenhearted and saves those who are crushed in spirit" (NIV). When I learned to approach God in the middle of my sinking, I was able to experience what it truly meant to be upheld by His righteous right hand (see Isa. 41:10).

Even though Proverbs 4:23 commands us to guard our hearts, the good news is that we don't have to do it alone. We have the power to renew our emotions with God as our counselor. When we cast our cares on God, He sustains us and refreshes us.

REFLECT + PRAY

Reflect

- What are the top two most common emotions you feel on a regular basis?
- What thoughts contribute to them the most?

Pray

- Ask the Lord what He would like to show you based on these feelings.
- Ask God to give you the ability to experience your feelings while also acknowledging His truth in the midst of them.

4. Follow-through | Revise Your Actions

How we respond to our internal framework is what I call **follow-through**. So often we follow through by reacting, not deciding.

Reactions are unintentional responses to our unreliable feelings.

In contrast, **decisions** are intentional commitments to our dependable faith.

Every day we have a choice. We can react according to the old, faulty frameworks that harm us, OR we can commit to the new, solid frameworks that free us. In other words, we can follow through on our feelings, or we can follow through on our faith.

Many Christian women have built habits upon their insecurities, which is why their lives don't produce the abundance that Christ promised. They struggle to bear "fruit" and exhaust themselves striving for all the wrong people.

Fruit is described in Matthew 7:17–20 this way:

A good tree produces good fruit, and a bad tree produces bad fruit. A good tree can't produce bad fruit, and a bad tree can't produce good fruit. So every tree that does not produce good fruit is chopped down and thrown into the fire. Yes, just as you can identify a tree by its fruit, so you can identify people by their actions.

In the same way that a tree is identified by its fruit, we are identified by our actions. As women pursuing confidence, we mustn't simply change our hearts; we must also change our habits. We accomplish this when we commit our actions to what God's Word says rather than responding to the way we feel.

But let's be real.

We won't always feel 100 percent confident in our faith. That would be ideal, but that's not honest. The good news, though, is that we can make these changes even before we fully believe this shift will improve our lives.

Imagine a Christian woman who wants to commit to celibacy before marriage even though she's been sexually active in the past. She may be operating out of fear and wondering, *What if I devote my body to God but I never find a man who will love and marry me without sex?*

Or ...

Imagine a smoker committing to breaking their cigarette addiction while questioning, *What if I relapse after a few months?*

Everyone will experience uncertainty before they make a major change in their lives. Uncertainty is normal when we attempt to change old habits. Why? Because those habits generated **certainty**. Smoking may not have led us in the best direction over the long term, but we could be CERTAIN that it would help quell our anxiety in the short term. Premarital sex may not have led us to our best life partner, but we could be CERTAIN it would give us some company for the moment and make us feel a little less alone in the world (while it lasted).

That kind of certainty might bring a little comfort, but it won't last long.

WE CAN FOLLOW THROUGH ON OUR FEELINGS, OR WE CAN FOLLOW THROUGH ON OUR FAITH.

I'll use myself as an example. When I ventured to lose the excess weight I'd gained during the pandemic shutdown of 2020, there were many moments when I craved the certainty of comfort that a pack of chips would bring. As a woman who loves food, I lusted after the certain delight that a dessert would bring ... *especially* when I was forfeiting **certain** gratification to pursue an **uncertain** goal. I had no idea if I'd really lose enough weight to make myself healthier, much less if I could keep it off for life.

However, even when I craved comfort, I remained committed. And because I committed, I conquered.

Over time, I lost every pound I'd gained and reached my goal weight by aligning my actions with that goal—even when I didn't feel like sticking to the plan. Even when I was uncertain about the outcome. Even when I was tempted by the immediate reward of feel-good foods. My decision to forego temporary certainty is what brought me lasting change.

This is the truth: we can commit to faith even when we don't feel it, and we can commit to what we *want to be true* before we fully *believe it's true.*

Yes, we can settle our deepest doubts with decision. And once we see our faithful follow-through producing fruitful feedback, we're able to accept the truth that what we do is who we become.

Action Supersedes Everything

Our action either disqualifies or reinforces our faith. If we act on a foreign principle often enough, then our beliefs, thoughts, and feelings will shift to welcome it. That's just how it works.

Now let's transfer this concept to confidence. If a woman doesn't feel confident, yet she consciously commits to ...

▸ saying what a confident woman would say,
▸ standing how a confident woman would stand,
▸ doing what a confident woman would do,

... then she will eventually **feel** like a confident woman and ultimately **become** a confident woman.

We really can act our way into feeling and behave our way into believing. For that reason, we should commit to confidence even when we don't yet feel confident. And the very decision to remain loyal to our commitments despite our doubts is what will confirm our confidence. Confident women don't always feel confident, but they still *choose* confidence. Therefore, they *are* confident.

Want to know an insider's tip? Here's a story about how I was able to choose confidence even when I felt insecure.

Years ago, I began focusing on what some might call "haters"— a few commenters who opposed me online. Even though thousands of women happily gleaned from the content I posted on YouTube, Instagram, TikTok, and Twitter, read the emails I sent to their inboxes, joined the groups I formed on Facebook, and enrolled in the programs I created on other platforms, I chose to dwell on the few commenters who bashed me, mischaracterized me, and directed negativity toward me.

I knew I was a genuine person who cared about others and was working to help them, and I was distraught that a minority of those I sought to reach saw me as an ingenuine fraud who only cared about herself. At times, I wanted to scream, *"I'm not who they think I am!"*

For a period of about six months, I unconsciously sank in insecurity. I would filter my content online to appear "nicer" and bend my honest convictions to emphasize how considerate I was of others. I subconsciously did these things with the hopes of being accepted as the genuine and caring person I knew myself to be. I didn't recognize that I was actually becoming *less* authentic by trying to present myself as *more* authentic.

What happened over time was … well, **nothing**.

No matter how much I bent over backward to be "understood" by strangers on the internet, they still teased me, judged me, and misunderstood me. The actions I took only ENHANCED my insecurities. I felt embarrassed and vulnerable every time I posted new content. This led me to consider abandoning sharing publicly on social media altogether, even though I knew God had called me to it.

After coming to a breaking point, I resolved to be confident in who God had called me to be despite what others assumed about my motives.

But I still felt wildly insecure.

After taking a long hiatus, I finally recorded a new episode of my podcast. But "fear of man" got the best of me yet again, and I deleted the episode the same night I uploaded it. I was too afraid of being picked apart.

Something had to give.

I knew I needed to change my mindset. So, after deep prayer and self-reflection, I uploaded the episode again, this time resisting the temptation to delete it.

You probably recognize this approach from what I've written so far. It worked for me, which is why I'm sharing it with you here. After that moment of transition, I began using the same approach when I posted on my other social media platforms. When overwhelming feelings of insecurity, embarrassment, and anxiety arose, I resolved to not alter what I was led to say or how I was led to say it. This process of follow-through was exactly the action I needed to take to overwhelm the fears that had once overwhelmed me.

DON'T BE FAITHFUL TO YOUR FEELINGS; BE FAITHFUL TO YOUR *FUTURE*.

But the change wasn't instant. In fact, I had to confront my fears over and over and over until I no longer caved to them. After months of aggressively confronting my fears with follow-through, I finally felt free. Free from the need to know what others were saying about me, free from the desire to correct every negative assumption about me, and free to follow what God was leading me to do.

Here's the lesson: your feelings won't change until *you* change. Don't be faithful to your feelings; be faithful to your **future**. Know that you're not going to feel confident before you are confident …

but show up anyway. Follow through in faith and let your feelings catch up.

Positive Actions That Will Cultivate Your Confidence

▸ Walk into environments with a tall posture, and hold your head up high.

▸ Make strong eye contact and choose open body language.

▸ Speak with a grounded tone that communicates certainty.

▸ Take leaps of faith in accordance with the Holy Spirit's prompting.

▸ Pursue opportunities you would have otherwise avoided.

▸ Commit to goals that will allow personal growth.

▸ Accept compliments by saying, "Thank you!"

▸ Put yourself "out there" to form new social connections.

▸ Ask for what you want and don't settle for less (e.g., pay, relationships, etc.).

▸ Celebrate your victories without minimizing them.

▸ Make decisions without wavering or second-guessing.

▸ Say no to things done from a place of obligation.

▸ Say yes to things aligned with your values and convictions.

▸ Do the thing that scares you.

You can take many actions that will communicate confidence to yourself and others. However, even when it comes to your ability to follow through on your faith, you can rejoice that you're never alone.

While unbelievers rely only on their own willpower to change, we get to rely on **God's power**. Romans 8:26–27 tells us that the Holy Spirit helps us in our weaknesses, intercedes for us, and gives our hearts the desire of the Spirit.

The Holy Spirit will help you to be faithful in the follow-through. You don't have to rely on your own strength to change; you get to rely on **God's strength**. This is why, even if you've built habits of insecurity, you can approach change with confidence. *What a gift!*

REFLECT + PRAY

Reflect

- What is the one action you can take that would make the biggest positive impact on your confidence?

Pray

- Thank the Lord for giving you the power to change by His Spirit.
- Ask Him to reveal how to align your actions with His will for your life, empowering you to remain committed despite uncertainty and insecurity.
- Ask Him to show you which things to say yes to and which things to say no to.
- Pray that He makes you faithful to communicate trust even when you struggle with doubt.
- Pray for Him to empower you through His Spirit to be faithful in the follow-through.

5. Feedback | Receive Your Reward

Like a return on investment, our input determines our output. The results that we produce—the good, bad, and in-between—provide **feedback** that helps us assess the quality of the effort that we input based on the data we gather from their output.

And guess what? God designed it this way.

Jeremiah 17:7–10 says,

> **Blessed are those who trust in the LORD**
> **and have made the LORD their hope and**
> **confidence.**
> They are like trees planted along a riverbank,
> with roots that reach deep into the water.
> Such trees are not bothered by the heat
> or worried by long months of drought.
> Their leaves stay green,
> and they never stop producing fruit.
>
> The human heart is the most deceitful of
> all things,
> and desperately wicked.
> Who really knows how bad it is?
> But I, the LORD, search all hearts
> and examine secret motives.
> **I give all people their due rewards,**
> **according to what their actions deserve.**

This passage of Scripture confirms that the feedback of our lives reveals where we've placed our faith—whether in humans or God. The object of our faith will dictate our rewards or consequences in life. God Himself will reward us when we place our confidence in Him.

Let's break this Scripture down to see this reward.

The Scripture begins, "Blessed are those who **trust** in the LORD." *Trust* can be translated as "**faith**." However, the sentence doesn't end by saying that we're blessed when we simply **trust**. It continues with the statement "**and have made** the LORD their hope and confidence."

The words *have made* are verbs, so they imply that **trust** results in **action**. It is when we pair faith with follow-through that we bear fruit.

The result? We become like "trees planted along a riverbank" with **deep roots**. Deep roots imply longevity and stability. Riverbanks can provide nourishment through soil and water. Therefore, we will be planted and rooted in the right environment for us to flourish.

We **won't be bothered by heat**. The idea of being unbothered by heat does not mean we won't feel the heat of life, but it does mean that what we feel won't faze us.

We also **won't be worried by drought**. This is because long months of drought are less threatening when a tree is rooted deep in *water*. Not only would it take long for the water to evaporate, but also—even if the water did evaporate—the water the tree has already stored within will withstand the dry season.

Therefore, our conscious effort to place our confidence in God enables us to triumph despite external circumstances that would otherwise destroy us.

IT IS WHEN WE PAIR FAITH WITH FOLLOW-THROUGH THAT WE BEAR FRUIT.

And finally, our **leaves remain green**—even in drought. In other words, we won't look like what we've been through. Heat and drought will come, but what is stored inside us overpowers whatever happens around us.

If we place our faith in human ability, we will be spiritually stunted and lack hope for our future. We won't have the internal infrastructure to withstand the weight of our external circumstances. But when we establish our **faith**, **focus**, **feelings**, and **follow-through** in God's ability, we will be sustained throughout hardship while spiritually flourishing.

What a beautiful promise.

In light of this promise, we must place our confidence entirely in the Lord. Believe in His goodness. Meditate upon His holiness. Speak His kindness. Feel His generosity. And respond to His faithfulness.

It is then that we will have sharpened our ability to stand in confidence.

REFLECT + PRAY

Reflect

- What are some results in your life that reflect the positive aspects of your belief systems?
- What results in your life reflect the unfavorable aspects of your belief systems?

Pray

- Thank the Lord for all the good things He has brought your way.
- Pray that He breathes on your efforts by blessing you with a fruitful harvest.

TAKE A STAND | RECLAIM YOUR CONFIDENCE

Reprogram Your Beliefs

For this exercise, you'll need a journal that has multiple pages available.

1. Review Your Faulty Faith

Write down four to seven limiting mentalities from your childhood that have programmed you to feel insecure. (NOTE: Place each mentality on its own page.) Next to each limiting belief, list its source(s).

Example of identifying the limiting mentality and source:

Mentality: "If I don't maintain a perfect body, then I will never find or deserve love."

Source: My father

Address the mentalities that have hindered you most in life.

2. Refute Your Faulty Faith

Underneath each mentality, challenge it with logical points that declare the truth. Use however many points you need to truly question the validity of your limiting belief. If you need to, research stories that refute your false narrative and build your faith.

Then challenge the credibility of the source based on evidence you may have, including Scripture.

Examples of challenging the limiting beliefs with truth:

▸ "Plenty of women have found romantic love who don't have what I've been told is a 'perfect body.'" (list names)

▸ "I already have perfect agape love through Christ, and my body doesn't determine that."

▸ "My body does not determine if I am worthy to receive love."

  • Matthew 6:25–30; Psalm 139:14; 1 Peter 3:3–4; Ephesians 1:4

▸ "My father's definition of love does not align with God's definition of love outlined by the life of Jesus and 1 Corinthians 13."

▸ "The only credible source for defining love is the Bible."

Renew Your Focus

Visualization is a powerful meditative tool to change thoughts and beliefs. This is done by generating mental images of a desired outcome. When we visualize ourselves living out the goal, we are training our minds and bodies for action long before we've ever lifted a finger.

For example, many Olympians say they've pictured themselves standing on that gold medal podium their entire lives. This is the same with many other "greats" who have achieved big goals.

They SAW it long before they LIVED it.

To renew your focus and embrace confidence, create mental imagery with your five senses to command your thoughts, words, and feelings.

1. Think about the Woman God Has Called You to Be

Paint a picture of who she is, being as detailed and descriptive as possible.

▸ What does she believe about God, and how does she relate to Him?

▸ What do her prayer, Bible study, and faith life look like?

▸ What does she use her words for?

▸ Who is she serving?

▸ What kind of relationships does she have?

▸ How does she treat others?

▸ How does she feel about herself?

▸ What does she wear that represents her?

▸ Where is she living?

▸ What is she doing on a daily basis?

▸ What goal is she working toward? What opportunities does she pursue?

▸ How does she respond to negativity, fear, and uncertainty?

▸ What kind of feedback is she receiving from the choices she makes?

2. Close Your Eyes and Visualize Being This Woman

Remain in this meditative state for five to ten minutes. The more frequently you do this visualization exercise, the more powerful it becomes.

For best results, do a three- to five-minute visualization every morning before you start your day.

3. Thank God in Prayer

Thank Him for empowering you to become who He has called you to be, believing that you are partnering with Him to become the woman you were born to be.

Renew Your Feelings

Remember, feelings are indicators that help us learn, grow, and find meaning. You will experience negative emotions because they are a normal part of life. But your negative emotions don't have to dictate your destiny. Use this exercise when you're experiencing negative feelings so that you can learn from and leverage your emotions to reclaim your confidence.

1. Identify Your Feelings

▸ Ask yourself, "What emotions am I feeling?"

▸ Ask, "What triggered my feelings?"

▸ Ask, "How do I want to respond to these feelings?"

2. Express Your Feelings

▸ Journal about your feelings.

▸ Vent to God about your feelings before venting to anyone else.

▸ Process your feelings with a friend, spouse, or therapist in the right context.

3. Learn from Your Feelings

▸ Ask yourself, "Why do I feel this way?"

▸ Ask God, "What are You showing me in the midst of these feelings?"

▸ Write down whatever is revealed, and then ask God for wisdom on how to respond.

Revise Your Actions

Since your habits shape your future, you will need to replace insecurity-based habits with confidence-cultivating habits. Charles Duhigg outlined a framework in his book *The Power of Habit*,[2] made up of three stages: **cue, routine, reward**. This habit cycle often happens automatically and unconsciously after the prompt triggers the action.

For the following forty-eight hours, you are going to observe ONE insecurity-based habit that you are seeking to change. After your observations, you will implement your revised habit cycle plan.

1. Study the Routine: During the next two days, write down in a journal the exact pattern that your habit follows. This is the behavior that you hope to change.

2. Identify the Cue: Note the moments when you feel compelled to perform a habit that feeds into your insecurities. Record every instance this urge arises.

3. Identify the Reward: Your habit will always have a payoff, which is the reward you were subconsciously craving. Record what the reward is.

4. Implement the Plan: After you've identified your habit cycle, it's time to devise a new plan. Here's how:

- Implement a **plan** to minimize the occurrence of the **cue**.
- Implement a new **routine** in response to the prompt when it does arise.
- Implement a new **reward** that is just as satisfying as the previous one.

Receive Your Reward

Following the **Reclaim Your Confidence Framework** may not be easy, but nothing of value ever really is. If you commit to making these exercises a part of your lifestyle, your end reward will be invaluable: finally being the confident woman that God created you to be.

Conviction

COMPONENT OF CONFIDENCE #4

The Necessity of Conviction

Conviction is the final component of confidence. Conviction is a fixed or firm belief. It is the state of being *convinced*. If we stand for anything, it is because of our conviction.

Think about it. All of the most powerful, influential leaders who lead movements and spark change have one thing in common: **conviction**.

Martin Luther King Jr. had a conviction. His belief in unity and justice drove him to lead a mass movement to seek racial equality that made ripples throughout history.

Of course, Adolf Hitler had a conviction too. His belief in the superiority of the German race is what drove him to lead a massive genocide against millions of Jews, Roma, Catholics, and other minority groups.

Both MLK Jr. and Hitler were so convinced in the magnitude of their causes that it led others to follow them—whether for good or for evil.

Jesus used His conviction to accomplish the ultimate good. Jesus was so deeply convicted to accomplish the Father's will of reconciling us back to Him that He was tortured on a cross as an innocent man. This sparked the genesis of the New Testament church and rescued generations from eternal damnation. Then Jesus commissioned us with a grave responsibility and an impenetrable authority.

This life isn't just about us. Others are following confident people who are leading them toward death, and we have been given the answer to life. We can't afford to waste our breath complaining, belittling, and undermining our God-given identity. Souls are at stake, and we have the power to help save them.

This responsibility and authority bestowed upon us is our "why." It is our driving force. It is the conviction that fuels us to take a stand.

The groundwork has already been laid. We have already established the **Clarity, Connection,** and **Competency** we need to stop sinking in insecurity. Now it's time to fan the flame of this **Conviction** by mastering the final two skills required to build confidence:

‣ **Know Your Responsibility** | Stand Firm
‣ **Use Your Authority** | Stand in Confidence

When you know your responsibility and use your authority, you will have the conviction you need to stand in confidence.

Chapter 7

KNOW YOUR RESPONSIBILITY

The Faces of Fear

I'm a risk-taker, a pioneer, and a nonconformist. I love the thrill of spontaneity and change, so I've **fearlessly** pounced on unusual and unexpected opportunities. This fearlessness has equipped me to marry, birth two kids, become a successful entrepreneur, and launch a ministry ... all by the age of twenty-four ... not to mention relocate to five different places before the age of twenty-eight!

Sure, peg me as moody, somber, and melancholy. But **fearful?** Pshh. *Nahhhh.*

At least that's what I thought ... until one day, during a therapy session, when my counselor asked me to indicate the fears that were driving my negative beliefs and emotions.

At first, I excused myself from the activity. *Fear is not my thing.* But at some point, I had to be honest with myself: If fear wasn't what was motivating me to shrink or strive, then what was?

My counselor helped me realize that fear doesn't always manifest as feeling nervous to launch a new business, appearing sheepish and bashful in public, or having a compulsive need to mitigate risk. Fear can present itself as insecurity, passivity, control, hoarding, skepticism, avoidance, perfectionism, performance, and people-pleasing too. In fact, some of the most fear-filled people overcompensate by *appearing* to be extremely confident and fearless!

I soon learned to discern the voice of fear. When I'm tempted to sink into self-doubt and shame or tempted to overwork and perform, it's because I'm afraid! I'm afraid of being insignificant, judged, and hurt.

Since that awareness, I started seeing fear everywhere. I saw a culture oppressed by fear. News channels are rated by their ability to incite fear. The ideological tribalism plaguing the internet and dividing our nation is a manifestation of fear. The women I mentored were fueled by fear. Even the people who hurt me were motivated by fear.

Fear had been the "man behind the curtain" all along. Yes, fear was the villain. Everyone, its victim.

The spirit of fear functions as a broker for Satan, and it comes to steal and to lie. In the garden of Eden, Adam and Eve found the spirit of fear disguised as the lure of possibility and suggestion. The possibility made them question, "What if I'm missing out on more?" The suggestion led them to wonder, "Is God truly who He says He is?"

Just as that the spirit of fear fraudulently persuaded Adam and Eve to abandon their faith, it does the same to us.

Do any of these fear-based scripts ring a bell?

The Social Anxiety Script: "You're being judged and you're going to get rejected. Stop believing in God to supply your relationships, and start concerning yourself with everyone's perception of you. Insecurity will keep you much safer."

The Doubter Script: "You're not very impactful, and you'll never achieve your purpose. Stop believing that things will change for you, and start doubting. Doubt will protect you far more than getting your hopes up and facing disappointment ever will."

The Skeptic Script: "Lack and loss are inevitable. You're going to keep losing everything good that comes your way. So stop pursuing good in your life, and start questioning everything. Suspicion will guard you from gaining anything of value that you'll have to lose later."

The Avoidant Script: "You're going to face a lot of pain and hardship if you follow God's path. Stop believing that God's path will prosper you, and start anticipating pain. Avoidance will protect you from pain by deterring you from God's path."

The Perfectionist Script: "You might end up a bad person. Stop trusting that you're redeemed, and start stressing and obsessing over your imperfections. Your tiresome elimination of wrongs will comfort you more than Jesus' sacrifice will."

The Self-Reliant Script: "You might end up incapable and helpless if you trust. Stop relying on God's ability and knowledge, and start figuring out how to do it all on your own. Self-reliance will ensure your safety more than God-reliance ever will."

The Control-Freak Script: "You might end up powerless in a situation. So stop trusting in God to take care of it; worry and take control of it in your own strength. Asserting your power will keep you safer than trusting in God's power."

The Stonewall Script: "People are going to hurt you. So don't rely on God to sort out your relationships; instead, just hide your emotions so that no one can get close enough to hurt you."

The People-Pleaser Script: "You're only valuable when you benefit others. People will stop loving you if you're unavailable, so don't set up boundaries. Agreeing with and working for others will protect your relationships more than trusting God will."

The spirit of fear is the one rehearsing these scripts in your ear, soliciting you to sin by placing your faith in **fear** rather than in God. Don't feel ashamed if you've fallen for fear's sleazy scheme. Fear is Satan's best salesman, and you're not fear's only victim. *So many* believers lack confidence because they haven't been equipped with the conviction or comebacks to silence the voice of fear.

Maybe that's why "Fear not" is the most repeated command in the Bible. The good news is this: the more prepared you are, the stronger you'll stand. When you have an adamant conviction about your responsibility to God, then you can **stand firm** in the face of fear. This stance will keep you sturdy during temptation, trials, persecution, and hardship.

To *stand firm* means to "stand up or offer resistance to somebody or something" or "refuse to abandon one's opinion or belief."[1] Based on this working definition of *stand firm*, when we cave in to the face of fear, we abandon what is true. When we stand firm in the face of fear, we resist Satan's lies and vehemently cling to God's truth instead.

Jesus Knew His Responsibility

Jesus knew the Father, and that's what grounded Him during His assignment on earth. His proximity to the Father gave Him certainty about the power of His Word, crowning Jesus the most fearless man to ever live, even when He faced the most severe cruelties and injustices.

Think about it—how can you threaten a man who has nothing to lose by death but everything to gain? His death, although gruesome and gory, only elevated Jesus to a higher position of glory, honor, and authority. And because He got His instruction from the Father and preparation from the Scriptures, He stood firm.

Even when He was questioned and accused, when He was plotted against and betrayed, and when He was beaten and flogged, He stood firm. Acknowledging the triumphant fulfillment of Scripture, He was certain that the plan was good. He was fearless because **He knew**—and no slander from a Sadducee, pander from a Pharisee, or deceit from a disciple could change the truth.

Jesus set the perfect example of what it looks like to stand firm. While His body was weak from fasting for forty days in the wilderness, His Spirit stood strong for the same reason (Matt. 4; Luke 4).

BECAUSE HE GOT HIS INSTRUCTION FROM THE FATHER AND PREPARATION FROM THE SCRIPTURES, HE STOOD FIRM.

Seeing Jesus in an interval of vulnerability, Satan came to seize the opportunity to overtake Him.

First, Satan appealed to Jesus' humanity by suggesting to Jesus, "Command that these stones become bread" (Matt. 4:3 NKJV). In offering the bread, Satan hoped to incite doubt, as if to say, "Are You sure the Father will supply all Your needs? Maybe after forty days, He'll let You die weak, hungry, and without." Satan tried to conceal fear within the suggestion of skepticism. Bread represented the **fear of lack**.

Jesus responded, "No! The Scriptures say, 'People do not live by bread alone, but by every word that comes from the mouth of God'" (v. 4). Jesus felt the humanity of hunger, yet He understood that He was more than His humanity. So rather than rehearsing His pain, He rehearsed God's truth. He didn't let a temporary moment of pleasure make Him lose sight of His lifetime of purpose.

Then Satan questioned Jesus' identity. He suggested that if Jesus were truly the Son of God, He could just throw Himself off the temple; of course angels would catch Him if He were truly God's Son.

Jesus wasn't fazed by the pressure to prove Himself to Satan. Because He knew the Father, He also knew who He was in relation to Him—His Son. Confident in His identity, Jesus responded, "The Scriptures also say, 'You must not test the LORD your God'" (v. 7).

Last, Satan tested Jesus' humility. He took Jesus up to a high place, showed Him all the kingdoms of the world, and said, "If You will kneel down and worship me, I will give You all of this" (see v. 9). Isn't it funny that the Enemy tested Jesus with what He was already destined to have?

While He was destined to rule in authority, Jesus had the humility to wait for it. He understood that the right thing at the wrong time is the wrong thing. Confident in the goodness of the Father and His plan, Jesus didn't entertain the possibility of expediting it. Again, Jesus responded, "The Scriptures say, 'You must worship the LORD your God and serve only him'" (v. 10).

After those indisputable comebacks, Satan had no scripts left to rehearse. So he left.

Jesus knew the Father, which gave Him conviction, and He knew the Scriptures, which prepared Him with comebacks to counter the spirit of fear. In the same way, you have to decide in advance how you're going to respond in the face of fear.

I have a theory. I think Satan tries to intimidate us because he's intimidated. I think he's the one who is dominated by the spirit of fear. He's afraid of what will happen once we assume authority over him and his repulsive demons.

If there's a chance that the Devil wants you to fear, then I think it's worth giving him a taste of his own medicine. The next time the Enemy reminds you of your past, flip the script and remind him of his future: "You and your demons will be thrown into the fiery lake of burning sulfur, where you will be tormented day and night forever and ever."

Face Your Fears

Like Jesus, we must know our responsibility and face our fears. In times of temptation, the Word of God gives us the comebacks we need to cause the Enemy to flee.

Use this section as a resource the next time you're facing fear, temptation, trials, or hardship of any kind. Based on the scripts we reviewed previously that will tempt you to falter, these counterscripts will equip you with conviction and provide comebacks to help you stand firm.

IN TIMES OF TEMPTATION, THE WORD OF GOD GIVES US THE COMEBACKS WE NEED TO CAUSE THE ENEMY TO FLEE.

The Social Anxiety Script

Conviction:

God is for me and not against me. He is a good Father who will give me good gifts, including the gift of the right relationships.

Comebacks:

▸ "[I] can say with confidence, 'The LORD is my helper, so I will have no fear. What can mere people do to me?'" (Heb. 13:6)

▸ "Fearing people is a dangerous trap, but trusting the LORD means safety." (Prov. 29:25)

▸ "Be strong and courageous! Do not be afraid and do not panic before them. For the LORD your God will personally go ahead of you. He will neither fail you nor abandon you." (Deut. 31:6)

The Doubter Script

Conviction:

God doesn't create anything without a purpose for it. I can trust that He will accomplish His perfect plan through me in His timing.

Comebacks:

▸ "It is impossible to please God without faith." (Heb. 11:6)

▸ "We are God's masterpiece. He has created us anew in Christ Jesus, so we can do the good things he planned for us long ago." (Eph. 2:10)

▸ "I tell you the truth, if you have faith and don't doubt, you can do things like this and much more. You can even say to this mountain, 'May you be lifted up and thrown into the sea,' and it will happen. You can pray for anything, and if you have faith, you will receive it." (Matt. 21:21–22)

The Skeptic Script

Conviction:

My Father is a God of restoration, and His ability to bless me is limitless. He is my provider and my sustainer. He is a good shepherd who sends goodness and mercy to follow me.

Comebacks:

▸ "The LORD God is our sun and our shield. He gives us grace and glory. The LORD will withhold no good thing from those who do what is right." (Ps. 84:11)

▸ "God will generously provide all you need. Then you will always have everything you need and plenty left over to share with others." (2 Cor. 9:8)

▸ "The thief's purpose is to steal and kill and destroy. My purpose is to give them a rich and satisfying life." (John 10:10)

The Avoidant Script

Conviction:

God will use all things for my good—including pain and hardship. I trust that if hard times come, He is developing me and producing within me a greater anointing for His glory. Because my Father is with me, I won't fear or avoid pain; I'll embrace it.

Comebacks:

▸ "I am willing to endure anything if it will bring salvation and eternal glory in Christ Jesus to those God has chosen. This is a trustworthy saying: If we die with him, we will also live with him. If we endure hardship, we will reign with him." (2 Tim. 2:10–12)

▸ "Dear brothers and sisters, when troubles of any kind come your way, consider it an opportunity for great joy. For you know that when your faith is tested, your endurance has a chance to grow." (James 1:2–3)

▸ "God blesses those who patiently endure testing and temptation. Afterward they will receive the crown of life that God has promised to those who love him." (James 1:12)

The Perfectionist Script

Conviction:

My Father is so kind and merciful that He sent Jesus to be perfect in my place. I don't need to be perfect to be acceptable; I just need to place my faith in Jesus, who makes me holy through His sacrifice, His Spirit, and His love.

Comebacks:

- "We who worship by the Spirit of God are the ones who are truly circumcised. We rely on what Christ Jesus has done for us. We put no confidence in human effort." (Phil. 3:3)
- "We are made right with God by placing our faith in Jesus Christ. And this is true for everyone who believes, no matter who we are." (Rom. 3:22)
- "My old self has been crucified with Christ. It is no longer I who live, but Christ lives in me." (Gal. 2:20)

The Self-Reliant Script

Conviction:

My Father is strong and able. He sends the Holy Spirit as my helper and my advocate to fight my battles for me. I don't have to depend on my ability because I can depend on His ability.

Comebacks:

- "'My grace is all you need. My power works best in weakness.' So now I am glad to boast about my weaknesses, so that the power of Christ can work through me." (2 Cor. 12:9)
- "He gives power to the weak and strength to the powerless. Even youths will become weak and tired, and young

men will fall in exhaustion. But those who trust in the LORD will find new strength. They will soar high on wings like eagles. They will run and not grow weary. They will walk and not faint." (Isa. 40:29–31)

The Control-Freak Script

Conviction:

My Father is in control, and I am not. Instead of overworking, I can rest in His divine plan. If someone overtakes me, I trust that God will avenge me.

Comebacks:

- "Jesus said, 'Come to me, all of you who are weary and carry heavy burdens, and I will give you rest.'" (Matt. 11:28)
- "Seek the Kingdom of God above all else, and live righteously, and he will give you everything you need." (Matt. 6:33)
- "I pray that God, the source of hope, will fill you completely with joy and peace because you trust in him. Then you will overflow with confident hope through the power of the Holy Spirit." (Rom. 15:13)

The Stonewall Script

Conviction:

My Father is with me and comforts me. I don't have to worry or hide my emotions because He will comfort me if I'm hurt, and He will protect me from harm. He will avenge me for all wrong done to me.

Comebacks:

▸ "Dear friends, never take revenge. Leave that to the righteous anger of God. For the Scriptures say, 'I will take revenge; I will pay them back,' says the LORD." (Rom. 12:19)

▸ "I have told you all this so that you may have peace in me. Here on earth you will have many trials and sorrows. But take heart, because I have overcome the world." (John 16:33)

▸ "Don't worry about anything; instead, pray about everything. Tell God what you need, and thank him for all he has done." (Phil. 4:6)

The People-Pleaser Script

Conviction:

My Father has given me acceptance, worth, and value. When I serve others, I will do it as an outpouring of love and not as a tool to gain approval.

Comebacks:

▸ "Obviously, I'm not trying to win the approval of people, but of God. If pleasing people were my goal, I would not be Christ's servant." (Gal. 1:10)

▸ "We speak as messengers approved by God to be entrusted with the Good News. Our purpose is to please God, not people. He alone examines the motives of our hearts." (1 Thess. 2:4)

Keep the Faith

When you choose to flip the script, you gain the ability to stand firm in the face of fear. But what about standing firm in our faith ... even when hard times come?

Jesus prepared His disciples to stand firm in the face of persecution by telling them to "be as shrewd as snakes and harmless as doves" (Matt. 10:16). He gave the apostles the vital responsibility to spread the gospel and expose truth in a dark, depraved world.

Jesus knew they would be whipped, flogged, arrested, and betrayed. He knew their persecution would involve being hated, mocked, slandered, misjudged, and even martyred. He certainly didn't sugarcoat the facts, but He taught them not to fear the threats of people who would ravage their bodies. Instead, He told them to fear God, who alone has the supremacy to ravage the soul.

Then Jesus said, "But everyone who endures to the end will be saved" (Matt. 10:22).

Endure. What does "endures to the end" mean?

In this verse, the word for "endure" is the Greek word *hupo-menó*,[2] and in similar Scriptures its cognate, *hupomoné*. This comes from the word *hypó*, literally translated "under," and *ménō*, meaning "to remain."[3] This is the same word for "persevere" in James 1:12, which reads, "Blessed is the one who **perseveres** under trial because, having stood the test, that person will receive the crown of life that the Lord has promised to those who love him" (NIV).

In other words, our endurance to the end will grant us salvation, and our perseverance under the weight of life's trials, tribulations, and temptations will grant us an eternal reward.

Now, I can guess where your mind is wandering. You're likely questioning, "Isn't salvation by **grace** through faith? It's not through my own work, right?"

The answer is *yes*, that's true. But you must *keep the faith*. Enduring to the end means **believing** to the end. **Trusting** to the end. And as belief shapes your behavior, genuine faith leads to faithfulness. If you say you have faith, then that same faith will keep you faithful even under the weight of life's most difficult circumstances.

Let's take marriage as an example. This covenant of enduring love is consummated when husband and wife say "I do." When a husband's personality shifts during a season of work stress, the wife continues to believe *he's still the one*. When the couple faces financial hardship, they hold on to the hope that hardship endured together is better than suffering apart. In their old age, when the wife gets diagnosed with terminal cancer, the husband stays by her side, remaining faithful to her until her last breath.

Their commitment to the covenant of marriage through life's trials proves that their love is genuine all the way to the end.

In the same way, your faith in God will cultivate adoration for Him. Love is the action that confirms your true affections. If your affection is set on money, then you will pursue it with all your heart. If your affection is set on fame, you will stop at nothing to get it. If your affection is set on Christ, then you will seek Him, and you will find Him.

YOUR FAITH IN GOD WILL
CULTIVATE ADORATION FOR HIM.

According to the Scriptures, love isn't love unless it bears all things, believes all things, hopes all things, **endures** all things (see 1 Cor. 13:7). This hopeful endurance keeps our covenant, evidencing our faith and proving our love.

Responsibility to Endure

When we stand our ground, it always works in our favor. Hebrews 12:1–2 says,

> And let us run with **endurance** the race God has set before us. We do this by keeping our eyes on **Jesus**, the champion who initiates and perfects our faith. Because of the joy awaiting him, he endured the cross, disregarding its shame. Now he is seated in the place of honor beside God's throne.

I treasure these verses with everything in me.

They tell us that Jesus is our *champion*. He is the One who starts and sustains us until the very end. Because His mind was set on the hope of our redemption, He was able to willingly withstand the most gruesome, torturous death. His long-suffering agony was facilitated entirely by His love. And because He endured, He was **exalted**.

After three days in the grave, Jesus was elevated to the highest point in all the heavens and earth—all by the sustaining, enduring, and abiding power of love. Now He reigns as the name above every name with all power and authority, and He will occupy the throne from everlasting to everlasting.

As Jesus modeled for us, let love be your confidence in the face of hardship, persecution, and temptation. With the joy set before you of your eternal inheritance, you can endure your cross.

Through adoration for your loving Father, you can ride out the most painful rejection, troubling disaster, and overwhelming chaos and still maintain your confidence.

Through the power of the Spirit living within you, there is no transition, no lack, no loss, no insecurity, no abuse, no injury, no illness, no failure, no threat, no persecution, no rejection, no condemnation, no shame, and no fear that will keep you from the love of God.

This is the confident hope that will give you the endurance to stand firm till your dying breath because not even death itself can separate you from the love of God.

The Purpose of Hard Times

Suffering serves a purpose. Suffering sanctifies us by strengthening our spirits while the flesh is weak.

Like gold being purified by fire, we are allowed suffering so that God can refine us into His likeness. More and more, you're conformed to the extravagant image of the Savior—and you shine all the more glorious because of it. Piece by piece, the impurities of sin, fear, insecurity, lies, and shame are sifted out. The result is that, like gold, your faith is proven to be genuine as you sparkle with beaming brilliance.

So it's not that we *have to* suffer; it's that we *get to*. Because even hard times have a promised hope: after you endure, you too will be exalted.

Scripture tells us that if we suffer with Christ, we will be **glorified** with Him (Rom. 8:17). It also says in 2 Timothy 2:12 that if we endure with Christ, then we will also **reign** with Him.

So in the same way that Christ humbled Himself as a servant and was lifted high in all splendor, we will be too. As you're willing to go low for the sake of Christ, He will take you high in His perfect timing. You will overcome in all brilliance, richness, and splendor if you stand firm. God has promised to do this for us in heaven, and He is more than willing and able to accomplish a microcosm of this triumph while still on earth.

TAKE A STAND | STAND FIRM

Now that the groundwork of **clarity**, **connection**, and **competency** has been laid, it's your responsibility to take a stand. You no longer have to work your way out of sinking. Now you simply need to **stand your ground with conviction**. Prepare your action plan with the steps below.

1. Identify the Script

Identify the script that the Enemy uses on you most.

2. Flip the Script

- Conviction: Make a list of three to five times God came through for you in this area.
- Comeback: Make a list of three to five Scriptures to combat the Enemy's script.

Use these lists to create your own script that you will rehearse whenever fear arises. It's best if you keep this script in your phone or somewhere that's accessible to you at all times.

3. Stand Firm

Write out a commitment to God, yourself, and others. This commitment will contain reasons that you choose to stand in confidence:

> ‣ What is your driving force to choose a life of confidence? What is your **why**?
> ‣ What's at stake if you don't take a stand for this conviction when fear arises?
> ‣ What is your responsibility to God, yourself, and others?
> ‣ Why is following God worth pursuing, even when you don't have to?

Write out a heartfelt commitment using these questions as a guide. Keep this commitment in your phone or somewhere that's accessible to you at all times. Use this commitment to anchor yourself and remind yourself of your responsibility to stand firm in the face of fear, temptation, and persecution.

Chapter 8

USE YOUR AUTHORITY

From Victim to Victor

A victim is only capable of being rescued, but a victor is tasked to rescue others.

Think about it—do you think it's possible for victims of insecurity to see beyond themselves to help someone else? *Absolutely not.*

A victim will always need to be saved and will never do the saving.

Similarly, the good news is not about Jesus reaching down to rescue you over and over again so that you remain perpetually helpless and pitiful. The good news is about Jesus giving you authority over your struggles and commissioning you to reach back to help rescue others.

The purpose of this book has been to shift you from a state of victimhood to a stance of victory. This chapter is the final step in that process, where I shake you up a bit to push you to stop feeling weak and powerless.

Counselors patiently work through our emotions with us, while **coaches** cut to the chase. They tell us the hard truths we need to hear to push us beyond emotion into **action**. Sure, we all could use some space to feel sad and pity ourselves, which helps us to process our pain adequately. I'm all for a good cry in the closet every now and then. However, at some point, we are obligated to stop licking our wounds and start challenging ourselves to grow.

There is a time to be counseled, and then there's a time to be coached. I'm the kind of person who likes to do both. I've done plenty of counseling throughout this book, so here's where I coach you into victory.

I have a responsibility to tell you the truth. So I'm going to shoot it to you straight.

Now that you've been given all the tools you need to stand in confidence, you no longer have any excuse not to.

THE GOOD NEWS IS ABOUT JESUS GIVING YOU AUTHORITY OVER YOUR STRUGGLES AND COMMISSIONING YOU TO REACH BACK TO HELP RESCUE OTHERS.

When we stand before Jesus to give an account of our lives, "insecurity" won't be a valid excuse for why we didn't accomplish what He called us to do. We won't be able to blame anyone else for what they did to us or how they didn't help us.

Whether something happened in your childhood, someone betrayed you, or you don't believe you can do it … none of those are valid excuses. You have been given all the tools and resources you need to pursue healing. You also have a present help in Christ, who gave you a new life.

Bad things have happened to you, yes. I'm sure life has been hard and painful and that those wounds have fueled your insecurities. But life has also happened FOR you. Everything you've been through has set you up for who you're called to be. And who you're called to reach.

So, at some point, it's time to stop identifying with victimhood and take authority over your life.

That doesn't mean you won't need help along the way. That's why I wrote this book for you. That's why you have the Holy Spirit. That's why you have counselors and pastors and other trusted mentors. While you may need help, you won't need rescuing. You've already been rescued.

Now it's your turn to go back and help others.

Reach Back to Rescue Others

The biggest tragedy is when someone who has already been rescued and who has already been given the resources to succeed refuses to change. Especially when they then take the focus off those who are the **real** victims.

There are real people in this world who don't know Jesus. There are real people out there who are lost. There are real people out there who are trapped in poverty, addiction, illness, or disability. Real people who are modern-day slaves sold into human trafficking. Real people who feel like they have no way out. People who are lost spiritually, emotionally, mentally, physically, and financially.

We're commissioned to direct our energy toward THEM.

We can't waste this life dependent on others to build us up.

We're called to be the ones building others up!

No one else is responsible to light us up ... WE are supposed to light others up.

Through Jesus, we are the light of the world! (John 8:12)

We can't afford to sink in insecurity. We have a responsibility—not only to ourselves—but to every person God has called us to reach.

Use Your Authority

There's no such thing as a confident victim. You're not going to be confident if you prophesy that you're always going to get the short end of the stick ... others are out to get you ... life is just more unfair to you than to others.

A mindset like that doesn't yield victory, or even align biblically. If you're going to **stand in confidence**, then you're going to need to break free from any traces of victimhood in your life and assume your authority in Christ.

So let's talk about what the Bible has to say about this.

You're Not a Victim to Sin.

1 Corinthians 10:13—No temptation has overtaken you except what is common to mankind. And God is faithful; he will not let you be tempted beyond what you can bear. But when you are tempted, he will also provide a way out so that you can endure it. (NIV)

Romans 6:14—Sin shall not have dominion over you, for you are not under law but under grace. (NKJV)

You're Not a Victim to Your Past.

2 Corinthians 5:17—If anyone is in Christ, he is a new creation; old things have passed away; behold, all things have become new. (NKJV)

You're Not a Victim to Your Circumstances.

James 1:2–4—Consider it pure joy, my brothers and sisters, whenever you face trials of many kinds, because you know that the testing of your faith produces perseverance. Let perseverance finish its work so that you may be mature and complete, not lacking anything. (NIV)

You're Not a Victim to This World.

1 John 5:4–5—Everyone born of God overcomes the world. This is the victory that has overcome the world, even our faith. Who is it that overcomes the world? Only the one who believes that Jesus is the Son of God. (NIV)

You're a child of God. *This is your identity and your inheritance in Christ!* But ... to whom much is given, much is required.

Remember who you once were? Remember how helpless you felt before God redeemed you? Do you see that there are far too many people around you who still feel just as lost and helpless? It's your turn to be the answer to their prayers.

IF YOU'RE GOING TO *STAND IN CONFIDENCE*, THEN YOU'RE GOING TO NEED TO BREAK FREE FROM ANY TRACES OF VICTIMHOOD IN YOUR LIFE AND ASSUME YOUR AUTHORITY IN CHRIST.

Will you let them drown in despair because you're preoccupied with your insecurities, or are you going to reach back, take them by the hand, and help them?

Let your conviction to help others override your doubts. You have an eternal responsibility to take a stand. They're depending on you.

REFLECT + PRAY

Reflect

- In what areas or scenarios have you taken on the attitude of a victim?
- In which areas are you taking on the attitude of a victor?
- Who is someone in need that you can reach back and help in some way?

Pray

Father, help me to see myself as victorious in all things. Empower me to use my authority to help others.

Eternal Perspective

It is our limited perspective that drives us to sink in hopelessness and victimhood. If the here and now seems too heavy to bear, we can begin to doubt that our efforts will make a difference. We may begin to wonder if our choices even matter at all. This is because, when our eyes are fixed on a particularly painful chapter in our lives, it's easy to lose sight of our ultimate purpose.

Therefore, the most compelling method to shift ourselves from victimhood to victory is to shift our viewpoint. We are going to set our sights on the chapter in our lives that will make standing in confidence worthwhile.

Some think that the most climactic chapter in our lives is our funeral. I believe that's incomplete.

The most climactic chapter in our lives is not the day that we die; it's the day that we meet Jesus. This end has already been pre-destined and prophesied, set in stone as the most epic event in the history of humanity.

We will *all* stand before Christ—whether in the great white throne judgment (Rev. 20 NKJV) or at the judgment seat of Christ (2 Cor. 5:9–11; Rom. 14:10–12). The former is a place of condemnation, and the latter is a place of celebration. Then each **believer** will stand before the judgment seat of Christ, like an athletic champion awaiting their medal.

At the judgment seat, those who lived their lives in light of this moment and did the Lord's work will be rewarded lavishly. The believers who lived for themselves will suffer loss but still will be saved—but "only as one escaping through the flames" (1 Cor. 3:15 NIV).

This moment is coming, whether we're prepared for it or not. Don't be mistaken—we all will give an account to Christ for the way we lived.

When we live with the end in mind, everything else comes into perspective. Knowing that we will one day stand before Jesus will shape the way we think, love, give, forgive, trust, and endure.

So, to conclude this book, I will paint a picture of what this day will be like. The imagery that I use will be biblical; however, no words I write will ever be able to adequately encompass what no eye has seen and no ear has heard.

Therefore, whatever words you read, picture the scene as even more magnificent. Let the destination of heaven be the lens through which you live your life and the compass that guides your decisions.

Do it all for the ultimate purpose: so that when you stand before Christ, you will **stand in confidence**.

The Final Chapter

The horn blares with a single, sustaining note. A declaration of deliverance. *It's happening.*

The world fades as you center your focus on the skies. Beaming with immaculate white light, the clouds inflate with the music.

At once, the winds, the tremors, and the sounds cease.

In the deafening silence, your heart races and you have just enough time to catch your breath before a thunderous voice shouts from above, "Behold: the Lord! The time has come when He will sit as judge! Fear and worship Him with the highest praise!" (see Rev. 14:7).

Suddenly, thousands of angels descend with gargantuan wing-spans, stirring movement back into the air. Firebolts crackle and clouds open wide as the Lamb of God is unveiled, robed in light that is purer and brighter than any you've seen before.

Jesus is here.

And He's coming for you!

In a blink, a servant angel lifts you into heaven. You hear the music of jubilee ringing throughout the cosmos. You smell the perfume of life everlasting. You see light, color, and matter more clearly and dynamic than ever before.

Your Savior stands before you. His hair is white, white as snow, and His eyes are a flame of fire. He shines with holy incandescence so bright that you can hardly behold His face. And yet—He looks at you with kind eyes and a tender smile. You are wrapped in a warmth of comfort, belonging, and love. This is the moment you've been anticipating.

Here stands the One you pray to and worship. This is the Lamb who laid down His life to ransom you. Gently He says, "I love you."

Crying, you fall to your knees in reverence as you worship Him with the highest praise. Then Jesus calls your name.

"Stand on your feet, and I will speak to you," Jesus says, and at once, the Spirit sets you firmly on your feet. With His arms open, He declares, "Child of God, your name is written in My Book of Life. Your sins are forgotten! Overwhelming victory is yours! Heaven belongs to you!" (see Rom. 8:37; Rev. 3:5; 20:12; 21:27).

Without thinking twice, you throw yourself into the arms of Jesus. He embraces you warmly with no rush.

Immediately, you feel unified with Him. His love becomes a tangible force, oscillating around you as it binds you to Him. You're exactly where you need to be, and nothing else matters. You're welcomed and loved beyond your wildest imagination. There's nothing you could have done to merit such an endowment. It's magnificent. It's extravagant. It's lavish. It's grace.

None of your sins are remembered. Rejection, condemnation, and shame are nowhere to be found.

"It's time for you to receive your inheritance," Jesus says. "Your physical body can't behold My glory, so you'll be given a new one" (see 2 Cor. 5:1–9).

Your jaw drops as you're transformed into a spiritual, heavenly body. Exquisite, fine linen adorns your body like a wedding gown. In the same way that Christ emits light, so do you. It's so beautiful.

Your eyes light up. *Could this get any better?*

"Oh, it gets better," Jesus replies.

"Come with Me." Instantly Jesus teleports you to an ornate platform that is mounted by steps. You don't see Jesus, but you sense His presence. You become aware of the multitudes surrounding you, more numerous than the grains of sand on a beach.

Then, like surround sound, you hear Jesus declare, "All must appear before the judgment seat of Christ! My reward is with Me, and I will recompense every person according to their deeds!" (see vv. 9–11).

A sense of confidence overtakes you.

You've been living your life; now is your opportunity to take your stand. You considered your life—you trusted God with little and much. When God told you to go, you went; to speak, you spoke. Even when you were tempted, Christ was your hope and His Spirit was your freedom. When you were tempted to seek another way, you stood in Jesus. When you wanted acceptance, you stood in love.

You weren't perfect, but by His power, you were faithful. You chose to **stand in confidence**.

In an instant, your life flashes before your eyes. You observe your life from birth until this point, sparing no breath. You see it all. And it all makes sense.

At this realization, Jesus takes you out of the visual, restoring you to the platform.

"I will reward you on account of your endurance," Jesus continues. "When you were tested, you endured. When you suffered, you kept the faith. You are like an olive tree, thriving in the house of God, trusting in My unfailing love. You are My special possession and My virtuous remnant! Come and receive the crown of life!" (see James 1:12; Rev. 2:10).

Jesus crowns you with a stunning royal diadem that brilliantly showcases the Father's satisfaction. The glory of this moment far exceeds all the loss you've suffered and all the pain you've endured.

Euphoria spills over you.

When the judgment is complete, the Lamb of God declares, "You will descend with Me into the Holy City to judge and reign with Me as My priest! Now join Me in the wedding feast!"

You consider every insecurity you once had, every fear that once guided you, and the undeserving feelings that once oppressed you. You remember the people who hurt you, the sacrifices you made, and the struggles you endured.

Seated in the cosmos with glory and majesty, joined by the Lord's presence ... it all seems so small. *What was there ever to fear?*

At last, you think to yourself, *How much more confident would I have been on earth if I had been living with this final chapter in mind?*

REFLECT + PRAY

Reflect

- When you stand before Jesus to receive salvation and to be rewarded for the life you lived on earth, how do you want to feel?
- What choices can you make each day that will ensure you feel that way when the day comes?

Pray

- Thank the Lord for the gift of life in Him.
- Ask Him to give you an eternal perspective that shapes your daily posture.
- Ask for a deeper hope and confidence in Him, the author and perfector of your faith.

STAND IN CONFIDENCE

Even the most confident believers will at times be approached by doubt, uncertainty, and insecurity. But how we stand our ground will make all the difference.

Teaching confidence doesn't exempt me from moments of insecurity. The other day, I was feeling less than confident about my body after having kids. This left me with the option to sink into vain insecurity or to remain standing in my identity.

Then I read a passage in 2 Corinthians 5 about Christ giving us our new, glorified bodies at the resurrection. Rather than finding ways to feel better about my current appearance, I was challenged to think bigger. To zoom out from the microscope of the here and now and see the big picture.

Gazing through the wide-angle lens of eternity, I saw that this life isn't my only hope. This body, not my only body. This home, not my forever home. In Christ, I have so much more to look forward to.

I zoomed so far out that I was no longer the focal point. The way my body looked in the mirror seemed so miniscule in view of the spectacle of God's plan. The Scripture was a sobering reminder that I will stand before Christ in the end, and when I do ... I want to be able to say that I wasn't distracted by the ancillary cares of life. I was fixated on **Him.**

In a matter of minutes, I felt confident again. Not because my body had changed, but because my focus did. When the Enemy was attempting to distract me from my mission, I was able to stand my ground in Christ by focusing *on Christ.*

The same is true for you. Being confident in Christ doesn't mean you'll never feel moments of insecurity. Your confidence will be shown not in whether those negative feelings arise, but in how you respond when they do.

YOU'LL BELIEVE YOU ARE WHO GOD SAYS YOU ARE BECAUSE GOD IS WHO HE SAYS HE IS.

So I'll leave you with this: When doubt, fear, uncertainty, and insecurity arise ...

Focus *on Him.*

The more you magnify yourself, the more you'll see insufficiencies and inadequacies.

As you hone in on Christ, you'll behold His infinite power and supreme glory.

You'll believe you are who God says you are because God is who He says He is. You'll trust that you'll do all that God has called you to do because He has done all He said He would do.

In Him is your clarity.

In Him is your connection.

In Him is your competency.

In Him is your conviction.

In Christ is your confidence.

ACKNOWLEDGMENTS

To my husband, Michael:

If only people knew. If only they knew that nearly all of my best ideas have come from you. That *you* were the one all those years ago who encouraged me to publish the post. Write the blog. Upload the video. Preach the sermon. *Put myself out there.*

Yes, it has always been you.

Your sheer presence in my life raised the standard for what I thought was possible. After so many faulty examples, you showed me what true love is. This introduction to genuine love was what pushed me closer to Christ and set the foundation of unshakable confidence in my life. I can say with integrity that I am a confident woman because you are a confident man.

To top it all off, you held it down with the kids as I locked myself in a room to hear the voice of God, flesh out my ideas, and write. Because you've blessed me, I can bless others.

You know these things, yet you never brag. You've pulled me higher without ever looking down on me. Thank you, best friend. I wouldn't reach my potential without you.

To the publishing team:

I'm immensely grateful for my publishing agent Alexander Field, and for the David C Cook team: acquisitions editor Susan McPherson, developmental editor Julie Cantrell, and the rest of the team. Thank you for believing in me and the vision of this book. You have been nothing short of welcoming, supportive, patient, and kind. We were able to bring this work to life because of you.

To God:

You've never been absent, and that's the best part. I haven't had to write any of this book in my own strength, my own wit, or my own might. This is all through You, with You, and for You. Forever and always, thank You.

NOTES

Chapter 1: Embrace Your Identity

1. Michael J. Pittman, "Why I Don't Love My Fiance," *Michael J. Pittman* (blog), February 11, 2014, https://michaeljpittman.wordpress.com/2014/02/11/why-i-dont-love-my-fiance.

Chapter 2: Define Your Design

1. Rick Warren, "Shaped for Serving God," in *The Purpose Driven Life: What on Earth Am I Here For?* (Grand Rapids, MI: Zondervan, 2002), 236.

2. Insights into these twelve gifts are aided by *Strong's Concordance*, Bible Hub, accessed December 2021, www.biblehub.com/strongs.htm, and Don Stewart, "What Are Spiritual Gifts?," Blue Letter Bible, accessed December 2021, www.blueletterbible.org/Comm/stewart_don/faq/introduction-to-the-gifts-of-the-holy-spirit/03-what-are-spiritual-gifts.cfm.

3. University of Zurich, "Every Person Has a Unique Brain Anatomy," ScienceDaily, July 10, 2018, www.sciencedaily.com/releases/2018/07/180710104631.htm.

4. "Matthew 7:24," Bible Hub, accessed December 2021, https://biblehub.com/interlinear/matthew/7-24.htm.

Chapter 3: Connect with God

1. John Piper, "All Things Are Yours: Bethlehem College and Seminary Commencement," desiringGod, May 17, 2013, www.desiringgod.org /messages/all-things-are-yours.

2. Mark E. Thibodeaux, *Armchair Mystic: Easing into Contemplative Prayer* (Cincinnati: St. Anthony Messenger Press, 2001).

3. "3056. logos," *Strong's Concordance*, Bible Hub, accessed December 2021, https://biblehub.com/greek/3056.htm.

4. "4487. rhéma," *Strong's Concordance*, Bible Hub, accessed December 2021, https://biblehub.com/greek/4487.htm.

Chapter 4: Connect with Others

1. "Strong Backs, Soft Fronts, and Wild Hearts with Brené Brown," Brené Brown, November 4, 2020, https://brenebrown.com/podcast /brene-on-strong-backs-soft-fronts-and-wild-hearts.

Chapter 5: Expand Your Capacity

1. Some of the ideas about healing in this chapter are drawn from Amanda D. Pittman, *CHANGE: Shed What Was Never You to Reveal Who You've Always Been* (self-pub., 2019).

2. Albert Wong, "Emotions Wheel," Dr. Albert Wong, accessed December 2021, www.dralbertwong.com/feelings-wheel.

Chapter 6: Sharpen Your Ability

1. For more on emotional intelligence, see "Emotional Intelligence," *Psychology Today*, accessed December 2021, www.psychologytoday.com /us/basics/emotional-intelligence.

2. Charles Duhigg, *The Power of Habit: Why We Do What We Do in Life and Business* (New York: Random House, 2014).

Chapter 7: Know Your Responsibility

1. The Free Dictionary, s.v. "stand firm," accessed December 2021, www.thefreedictionary.com/stand+firm.

2. "5278. hupomenó," *Strong's Concordance*, Bible Hub, accessed December 2021, https://biblehub.com/greek/5278.htm.

3. "5281. hupomoné," *Strong's Concordance*, Bible Hub, accessed December 2021, https://biblehub.com/greek/5281.htm.

RESOURCES

Brown, Gregory. "5. How to Battle Fear, Doubt, and Discouragement (Genesis 15:1–6)." Bible.org. July 10, 2017. https://bible.org/seriespage/5-how-battle-fear-doubt-and-discouragement-genesis-151-6.

Calvano, Gina. "Purpose vs. Calling—What's the Difference?" Indigoforce. July 9, 2012. http://indigoforce.com/345.

Clear, James. *Atomic Habits: An Easy & Proven Way to Build Good Habits & Break Bad Ones.* New York: Avery, 2018.

Clear, James. "How to Master the Invisible Hand That Shapes Our Lives." James Clear. https://jamesclear.com/feedback-loops.

Cloud, Henry. *Necessary Endings: The Employees, Businesses, and Relationships That All of Us Have to Give Up in Order to Move Forward.* New York: HarperCollins, 2011.

Daniels, Dharius. *Relational Intelligence: The People Skills You Need for the Life of Purpose You Want.* Grand Rapids, MI: Zondervan, 2020.

DiSC Profile. "What Is DiSC?" www.discprofile.com/what-is-disc.

Knopf, Eric. "Learn about the Fivefold Ministry." Fivefold Ministry Test. https://fivefoldministry.com/static/learn-about-the-five-fold-ministry.

Kreider, Larry. *Speak, Lord, I'm Listening: How to Hear God's Voice above the Noise.* Ventura, CA: Regal Books, 2008.

Krotoski, Aleks. "Robin Dunbar: We Can Only Ever Have 150 Friends at Most ..." *The Guardian.* March 13, 2010. www.theguardian.com /technology/2010/mar/14/my-bright-idea-robin-dunbar.

May, Michelle. "Reprogram Your Brain." *HuffPost.* December 6, 2017. www.huffpost.com/entry/reprogram-your-brain_b_5515443.

The Myers & Briggs Foundation. "MBTI Basics." www.myersbriggs.org /my-mbti-personality-type/mbti-basics.

Pierce, Debbie. "Toxic Friendships: The Signs and Solutions." Life, Hope & Truth. https://lifehopeandtruth.com/relationships/friendship /toxic-friendships.

Pittman, Amanda D. "Who Is Jesus?" Confident Woman Co. 2019. www.confidentwomanco.com/jesus.

Praying Medic. *Emotional Healing in 3 Easy Steps.* Gilbert, AZ: Inkity Press, 2016.

About the Author

Amanda Pittman is a proud wife and mother of two. She is an author, ministry leader, speaker, and entrepreneur. Amanda is the founder of Confident Woman Co., a ministry that uses online challenges and groups, live events, and more to equip women to stand confidently upon the finished work of Jesus.

www.confidentwomanco.com
www.amandaapittman.com